Praise for

DON'T READ POETRY

"An inviting guide to an art form often seen as abstruse....At once erudite and colloquial, the book resists prescriptive judgments, teems with surprising juxtapositions, and evokes the contagious enthusiasm of a cool teacher."

—*New Yorker*

"Charming...Burt is a delightful companion who reminds us that poems go down a lot better if we read them out loud and slowly....The whole idea of *Don't Read Poetry* is not only to celebrate the freedom and inventiveness in poems...but also to connect poems to a larger world of beauty."

—*Christian Science Monitor*

"Burt is well-suited to convince even the most skeptical readers that poems, indeed, should be read by everybody."

—*Booklist* (starred review)

"In this eloquent literary primer, Burt...contends with poetry's reputation for inaccessibility....[A] sweeping, insightful survey."

—*Publishers Weekly*

"*Don't Read Poetry* is for readers hunting sharp, nimble thinking about culture, comprehension, and poems. Whether discussing an ancestral Hawaiian language, a canonical poet like Langston Hughes, or contemporary poets like Rodrigo Toscano and Jennifer Chang, Stephanie Burt manages to illuminate 'the difficult process of turning paired marks into words.' Don't read poetry, she suggests, read poems. This is a book for anyone who reads with curiosity, care, and imagination."

—Terrance Hayes, author of *American Sonnets for My Past and Future Assassin*

"When I began Stephanie Burt's *Don't Read Poetry*, I fully expected her to widen and deepen my appreciation of this art form. Burt is, after all, a masterful poet, teacher, and literary critic. What I didn't necessarily expect was that I'd have such a great time absorbing what she has to say. Whether you love poetry or resist it, you will enjoy this entertaining and enlightening book."

—Wally Lamb, author of *I Know This Much Is True*

"For the past fifty years, poetry critics have battled over what poetry is, which poets mattered, and which didn't. Stephanie Burt says they had it wrong. Don't read poetry, this dedicated pluralist tells us, if by poetry you mean one thing. If however you want to read poems, and discover the manifold ways they can be—and help readers to be—good (for Burt's aesthetic vision is ultimately ethical), read this lucid, informed, and deeply humane book."

—Langdon Hammer, author of *James Merrill: Life and Art*

DON'T
READ
POETRY

DON'T READ POETRY

A BOOK ABOUT HOW TO READ POEMS

STEPHANIE BURT

BASIC BOOKS
New York

Cover design by Chin-Yee Lai
Cover image copyright © Plainpicture / Reilika Landen
Cover copyright © 2023 Hachette Book Group, Inc.

Basic Books
Hachette Book Group
1290 Avenue of the Americas, New York, NY 10104
www.basicbooks.com

Printed in the United States of America

Originally published in hardcover and ebook by Basic Books in May 2019.
First Trade Paperback Edition: May 2023

Published by Basic Books, an imprint of Perseus Books, LLC, a subsidiary of Hachette Book Group, Inc. The Basic Books name and logo is a trademark of the Hachette Book Group.

The Hachette Speakers Bureau provides a wide range of authors for speaking events. To find out more, go to hachettespeakersbureau.com or email HachetteSpeakers@hbgusa.com.

Basic books may be purchased in bulk for business, educational, or promotional use. For more information, please contact your local bookseller or the Hachette Book Group Special Markets Department at special.markets@hbgusa.com.

The publisher is not responsible for websites (or their content) that are not owned by the publisher.

Print book interior design by Jeff Williams.

The Library of Congress has cataloged the hardcover edition as follows:
Names: Burt, Stephanie, author.
Title: Don't read poetry : a book about how to read poems / Stephanie Burt.
Description: First edition. | New York : Basic Books, 2019. | Includes index.
Identifiers: LCCN 2018054504| ISBN 9780465094509 (hardcover) | ISBN 9780465094516 (ebook)
Subjects: LCSH: American poetry—History and criticism. | English poetry—History and criticism | Poetry—Explication.
Classification: LCC PS303 .B86 2019 | DDC 811/.009—dc23
LC record available at https://lccn.loc.gov/2018054504

ISBNs: 9780465094509 (hardcover), 9780465094516 (ebook), 9781541603615 (paperback)

LSC-C

Printing 1, 2023

Cooper and Nathan and Jessie,
as always, for always

She isn't making noise for the sake of making noise. She's letting me inside her head, and for the first time in my life, I feel I can almost imagine it—what it'd be like to exist as a completely different person, to have their thoughts and feelings instead of my own.

—KHERYN CALLENDER, *HURRICANE CHILD*

Was that voice ourselves? Scraps, orts and fragments, are we, also, that?

—VIRGINIA WOOLF, *BETWEEN THE ACTS*

She needed a way to be sure it was her inside the machine.

—APRIL DANIELS, *DREADNOUGHT*

CONTENTS

READING POEMS

O F ALL THE KINDS OF ART THAT PEOPLE MAKE, POEMS are, or should be, the easiest to share, maybe even the easiest to find. They need not be read live, or on stage, or by their authors, or even aloud (though it helps); they require no musical instruments or playback devices. Some can be memorized; most can be collected, reprinted, copied out by hand, or shared via email; and most of them don't take very long to read.

So why don't more of us read more poems? Why do some people care so much about poems that baffle the rest of us? Why do the same people often loathe poems others like? Are poems from five hundred years ago really the same things—can they work on us in the same ways—as poems by living authors now? Do all sorts of poems work the same way? Have they always? How can the poems that are out there all deserve the label "poetry" when they seem so far apart?

This book tries to answer those questions. It gives not just ways to read poems but reasons to read them, and ways to connect the poets and poems of the past, from Sappho and Li Bai to Wordsworth to some poems being written right now. And it starts from the idea—which took me a while to realize was not obvious, or universal, or widely recognized in schools—that poems are like pieces of music: by definition they all have something in common, but they vary widely in how they work, where they come from, and what they try to do. Various readers like various poems for various reasons, just as various listeners like various genres of music, various artists, and various songs. And the same listener (you, for example) can care about different songs for different reasons, at different times in your life or even at different times of day.

I came to write this book in part because I've been teaching people how to like poems, and how to see why others like poems, since the early 1990s; I've also been writing about old and new poems for magazines since then, in what now adds up to several hundred essays and book reviews. But this is not a book of book reviews; it is, in a sense, an alternative to them, a way to show what I'm looking for (which may not be what you're looking for) when I flip through the hundreds of books of poetry that I get in the mail each year and the dozens I still go out of my way to buy, and when I find—as I do, more often each year—a poem I like a lot, by an author I've never heard of, on Twitter or Facebook or in a glossy quarterly or in a brand-new journal that exists only onscreen.

But it's not just me. Consider all the things that the word *poetry* can mean, and all the things that the various sets of words called poems can do.

Two teenagers in Singapore open their web browsers to a social media site and find there eight lines written four hundred years ago in England, quoted yesterday by another teen in Tasmania, about the persistence of friendship across time and space.

A superhero in an X-Men comic reads verse by Percy Bysshe Shelley aloud at her daughter's funeral; the superhero's colleague, a teacher, relaxes by rereading Robert Frost.

Dozens of lines in the alliterative meter and in the approximate style of the Old English heroic epic *Beowulf* adapt the plot of a television commercial for Old Spice deodorant, to hilarious effect; the parody achieves some popularity online.

At a funeral, a rabbi reads the Twenty-Third Psalm in a modern English version designed for Jewish liturgical use. Five time zones away, a pastor reads the same psalm to her congregation in the 1611 translation sponsored by King James; one of her congregants, fluent in both languages, considers the differences between the English and the biblical Hebrew.

A graduate student counts the number of times that William Butler Yeats uses the words *blood*, *love*, and *moon* in all his poems. Another proposes to her future wife by reading a Yeats poem out loud. A third compares translations into English of thousand-year-old poem-songs about sexual love and devotion from the South Indian language Telugu.

An English professor delivers a lecture about Bob Dylan. Three doors down, another professor delivers another lecture about the rap artist and singer Angel Haze while, across campus in the music department, a third professor examines Lorenzo Da Ponte's choice of words for Mozart's *Così fan tutte*.

An inquisitive polymath admires the pattern of synonyms and antonyms and the contrasting pattern of ascending and descending lowercase letters in three pages of prose that make no literal sense.

An administrative assistant spends his lunch hour copying down Thomas Gray's "Elegy Written in a Country Church-yard"; another writes "I, too, dislike it"—the opening line of Marianne Moore's poem called "Poetry"— on a napkin during a meeting.

Two hundred people in a Portland nightclub watch one person on stage describe, in scary detail, their flight from their birth family and the new life they have just now been able to find. One month later the performance becomes available on a YouTube channel and fans transcribe it; a few recite it themselves. The next year the performer publishes the description, in verse, in a book that comes with a CD.

James Weldon Johnson's words to "Lift Ev'ry Voice and Sing" (sometimes referred to as the "Black National Anthem") are sung at a school assembly for the 998th time this year.

Middle-school students build a set for a staged reading of Edgar Lee Masters's *Spoon River Anthology*, in which each short work's speaker is a different deceased inhabitant of a small midwestern town.

A student learning to read and speak Chinese creates yet another English-language version of a quatrain by Li Bai about seeing the moon too far from home. Eighty years earlier, a Chinese immigrant detained at Angel Island in San Francisco Bay scratched the same quatrain on the wall of his cell; other inmates scratched other classic Chinese poems on other cell walls, sometimes adding new poetry of their own.

Elizabeth Bishop, already famous for her careful descriptive verse, changes the punctuation in the final draft of her villanelle about almost losing her lover, called "One Art."

An ancient Egyptian (their name now lost) writes down a few lines comparing their love to a goose, to a rosebud, to a flame, to a dove.

We can say that all these people are reading, or writing, or hearing poetry, but what would we mean by *poetry*? Until about two hundred years ago the word could mean "imaginative literature," anything made up, or not real, or not true in prose or verse. Now it means verse, or prose that feels like verse, or (sometimes) anything that feels elegant, moving, sublime, above-and-beyond, not quite of this world: athletes' shots and politicians' speeches and dance moves are said to be pure poetry, meaning that we admire their beauty or their sublimity but wonder if they have any practical use. Much-noticed and much-debated essays, going back at least two hundred years, with titles like "Can Poetry Matter?" and "The Four Ages of Poetry" (gold, silver, bronze, and iron), have argued that poetry is in decline, has long been in decline, because fewer people love Shakespeare or Dickinson or Homer or Robert Frost. Other essays, some with surveys to back them up, show that poetry is coming back, or never left: after all, look how many people now write it!

Look, too, at the communities that have formed, some within universities, some far outside them, around particular poems and ways to read poetry, from classrooms where kids love *The Odyssey* in new translations, to self-conscious avant-gardes in urban centers, to immigrant communities refreshing a heritage language and its verse forms. These readers and writers are not all reading the same poems, or reading in the same way, or for the same reasons. They're not all reading the same kinds of poems, and they may not agree on what counts as poetry, much less on what counts as good poetry.

And yet some of them—some of us, many of us; not just we readers of poems but we Americans (since I'm American), we readers of English, of anything at all—are caught in a myth about what counts as poetry and how we might learn to enjoy and to read it. The myth says that poetry is one thing and that poetry matters to us, or should matter, for one big reason. Maybe it introduces us to other people and other cultures, opening up our minds. Maybe it makes us more authentic and opens us up to ourselves. Maybe it brings us together as a country or as a community; maybe it used to do that, but it doesn't now, so poets had better change how we write poems.

Maybe it opens us up to the numinous, to the sacred, to the weird, to the unknown. Maybe it's a difficult art whose practitioners deserve plaudits for their pure technique, like show pilots who do loops and rolls in midair. (Maybe it's a form of verbal combat: poets, like fighter pilots, battle to rule the air.) Maybe it makes us feel warm inside or sustains our life's illusions; maybe it can bring the revolution, or (to quote W. H. Auden) "disenchant and disintoxicate." Maybe we need to learn about it in school—after all, poetry is old and complex and there are professors of it. Or maybe we can only learn the truth about poetry outside of school, since it's intuitive and instinctive and, as the Latin proverb says, "poets are born, not made" (nobody knows who made up the proverb). Maybe it's just a mystery that most people never get. Or maybe there are a few poems that will unlock it all for you; read them and you'll have the whole ball of wax.

I am here to say that anyone who tells you that they know how to read poetry, or what poetry really is, or what it is good for, or why you should read it, in general, is already getting it wrong. *Poetry*, the word, has many overlapping meanings, most of them about composition in verse; there are many such compositions, and many ways to write them, and many reasons to read them, and if you want to find or like or love or write more of them, the first thing to do is to start to tell them apart. Many people read poems for many reasons, and yours may not be your uncle's, or your best friend's, or your daughter's, or your professor's.

I started to write this book because I got frustrated with books that told their readers, and teachers who told their students, that poetry was one thing. Sometimes the readers and the students learned to love that thing; sometimes they tried it and decided that this one thing—this major poet (say, Robert Frost), this reason to read (say, mystery and the sacred), or this style of poetry (say, modern conversational free verse)—wasn't for them. That's like hearing Beethoven, or hearing Kendrick Lamar, and not getting into it and then deciding you don't like music. There are other kinds of music and other ways to listen to music out there, and if you look and listen and ask the right people, you can probably find one that works for you.

So: don't read poetry. Don't assume *poetry* ever means only one thing, other than maybe a set of tools for making things with words, as *music* means a set of tools (beats, rhythms, harmonies, textures, instruments) for making things with sounds. Instead, find ways to encounter kinds of poems and learn different reasons to read poems, realized in various ways by various poems. In this way, if in no other, poetry is like the New York City subway (albeit in slightly better repair). The subway system is always running and can take you almost anywhere in New York, but not all trains run at all times, and each train goes only to certain destinations. In the same way, lines of poetry can take you to many emotional places and to many parts of history and of the world today, but each line of poetry goes only to certain places, and what line you take depends on where you want to go.

Think of this book, then, almost as a partial map of an urban subway system, a big one like New York's. It's an attempt to show you, not the whole history of the system nor how all the trains work, but what train to take if you want to get where you are going, how you might find out about other places the system can take you, and, simply, how to ride. (Mostly it covers the parts of the poetry system written in English, since I am writing in English myself; there are branch lines that take you to other languages, which have their own systems in turn.) The system of poems can be a bit confusing at first, but it gets more comprehensible the more places you go; it's also cheap compared to other arts, or other means of transportation (like movies or opera, or private cars). It's forbidding if you're not used to it, and it's not for everyone (neither is New York City), but it's got a lot to recommend it once you know how to follow it and how to get inside.

•

Poem comes from an ancient Greek verb that means "to make"; medieval Scots called poets "makars," people who made things out of words. They shared not goals but techniques. If you want a definition for *poetry*, you may as well go to those techniques: patterns in sound (only some of those patterns have names), metaphors and other kinds of symbolism in language, ways to let language *do* things that cannot be straightforwardly, simply, *said*. Poems and poets make language their instrument—and they do various things with that instrument, as guitarists do with guitars, singers with their voices.

I read a lot of poetry as well as a lot of books about poetry. But I am writing this book first of all for people who do not, or do not yet, read nearly as much. It's for people who found "Meditations in an Emergency" by Frank O'Hara after hearing it on *Mad Men* or Percy Bysshe Shelley's "Ozymandias" after binge-watching *Breaking Bad*. It's also for people, most of them younger than I am, who are getting into poetry by watching poets' performances, live or on YouTube, or through their own and their friends' often very personal websites. The subjects of poems in live performance by the poet, and song lyrics that normally go with music, including hip-hop texts, will come up, but this is not a book about them: it's about texts you can read, without hearing someone else read them, about some things those texts can do.

People who talk about "poetry" in general—people whose tastes I may share but whose take on the art I want to counteract—tend to take it very seriously. So a cartoon analogy may help. If you (or someone in your house) play or watch Pokémon, you may be aware that there are a *lot* of Pokémon: small cartoon monsters that sometimes turn into one another, each with a different skill. Poems and poets differ in their abilities and their goals almost as much as Pokémon do, even though they exist in the same universe and follow the same basic rules: you might ask Wartortle to put out a fire, but if you want to start one, Charmander is the better choice. Similarly, we shouldn't hold poems that put out fires—that calm us down, let us escape daily life, or reassure us—in lower esteem than poems that start fires, or unsettle us, or challenge us: sometimes we need help calming down in a frightening world.

Jorie Graham's scary and wonderful modern poem "Region of Unlikeness" imagines a hostile questioner confronting her teenage self, demanding: "What is the purpose of poetry, friend?" But there is no one purpose to all poetry; there are only poems, lots of them, memorable and ridiculous and calm and volatile and heartbreaking and fascinating poems. Some of those poems tell us—seriously or jocularly or sarcastically or heartbreakingly—what poems must do and what poetry means, not for every poet who ever lived but for this poet, in this poem, now. And they may disagree. Auden entitled one of his poems (quoting Shakespeare) "The Truest Poetry Is the Most Feigning." Other readers and poets need poems to feign nothing and mean everything, to not take risks but to help them feel safe: the women in Hazel Hall's 1924 poem "Light Sleep" "lie in fear till day, / Clasping an amulet of words to keep / The leaning dark away." Jenny Bornholdt, in her long poem "Fitter Turner," comically compares the writing of poetry to physical therapy:

> After a lot of physio and lifting weights
> made from my father's socks filled with sand
>
> and draped over my ankle, my knee improved. It's years ago
> now, and although it still troubles me sometimes, mostly

it's all right. I'm not meant to run or play sports—like tennis or squash—which involve sudden changes of direction.

Poetry, being low impact, is fine.

That last sentence holds multiple deadpan jokes about the kind of poetry Bornholdt writes: it has little impact on most of the world ("Poetry makes nothing happen," as Auden wrote), and writing it isn't physically strenuous in the way that tennis is. Yet poetry *does* involve changes of direction, not least in the management of stanzas and lines. Each line can change your sense of what the last one meant and of where the poet wants you to go.

That is to say that different parts of the same poem—as well as different poems—can take you, in different ways, to different places. Poems—not "poetry" but individual poems—can bolster a civil rights movement, console the dying, congratulate new parents, introduce you to characters and settings you could never have imagined, help you quit your job or find a new one or live without one, give you pleasures like those you might get from crossword puzzles or sewing or watching basketball or playing basketball or accomplishing a mathematical proof, and (maybe most of all) show you that you're not alone.

Few poems can meet all those goals at once; to get all you can, and to find the poems you like, you'll have to accept that, as the English Renaissance poet and songwriter Thomas Campion put it, "all do not all things well." A poem that's great at one thing, for one reader, may appall or turn off someone else (Campion's poem turns out to be, in part, about how we don't all want the same thing from sex). In her book about singing, *Naked at the Albert Hall*, the singer and songwriter Tracey Thorn recalls how "our bass player . . . said to me years ago, 'You don't go to Frank Sinatra for the disco numbers, do you?'" She continues: "What do we want from singers? . . . We don't always want or need the same thing."

Nor do we need to know how to describe what we want before we can get it; we certainly do not need to know, in advance, the technical terms. Indeed, the experience of hearing or reading a poet's gift is why we care to learn (if we do) those terms. You can read poems for the wisdom, for the surprise, for the feeling, for the richness or the oddity of the language, without knowing anything at all about the history of poetic techniques. In the same way, you can follow a sport—say, basketball—and admire Lindsay Whalen's ability to know where all her teammates are or Steph Curry's talent for placing a ball in a hoop from far away without knowing a three-point line from a block/charge call. But if you like watching athletes exercise those talents, you might want to learn the rules and the history of their game.

I called this book *Don't Read Poetry* because if you are looking for reasons to read or write or defend one thing called poetry, you are probably already doing it wrong. There *is* a thing called poetry, a history of ways to arrange words that are not limited by those words' meanings, and that often involve (among other patterns) verse lines. In the same way, there is a thing called music in which tones and rhythms are produced, on purpose, in patterns, by human beings. But we don't listen to music so much as we listen to Beethoven or Beyoncé; we do not learn to cook in general but to cook pasta or omelets, bibimbap or pho. We do not play "sports" but play basketball or skate. And I do not read (or study or write or teach) poetry so much as I read and teach the work of individual poets, who write poems.

Those poems work in various ways toward various ends and give us various reasons to read them. Six of those reasons organize the chapters that make up the rest of this book.

First, *feelings*. Poems arrange language to convey, share, or provoke emotions, whatever else they do. It's hard to imagine a poem (but easy to imagine, say, a recipe or a guide to particle physics) whose ways of arranging language make you feel nothing at all above and beyond how you feel about the topic. When emotions, attitudes, shared feelings are the first or last or most important thing the words in a poem evoke—when they feel expressive, when they are more like songs we could sing than like pictures of people we could meet or stories we could tell—we can call that poem a *lyric poem*: not *lyrics*, sung words, but *lyric*, singular, meaning that its words (even without music) behave like the words in songs, sharing feelings an imagined voice might convey. Auden also called poetry, in general, as he read it, "the clear expression of mixed feelings," and this chapter will show why some poems fit those words.

Second, *characters*. Poems can introduce us to imagined people, or characters, much like or very unlike us. Novels, films, plays, and epic and narrative poems can show characters in action, letting people (or robots or talking animals) show us who they really are by showing us what they do. Short poems, like most of those discussed in this book, can show us, instead, who somebody is at one moment, conveying an individual's

13

character in arrangements of language. We will find out how poets construct characters who are definitely not the poet, who may speak and behave as if onstage. We will also see how poets portray themselves as recognizable characters in their own poems, and why so many poems imagine that animals, plants, and inanimate objects can talk.

Third, *technique*. Some poems feel raw, like spontaneous speech, but others put forward careful and intricate shapes. Such poems can give pleasure just for the sake of those shapes, the pleasures of following anything that requires exceptional skill, or of watching a puzzle get solved. Some poets make up forms from scratch. Others adopt and adapt old forms for new conditions, showing in the process that old forms need not always sound old, or European, or white.

Some poets solve complex problems; others present *us* with problems, in poems that stand out—and appeal to some readers—for *difficulty*, the subject of chapter 4. Such poems' opaque or resistant or even aggressive language can work to break up the habits that we carry with us into the world beyond poems; they may enliven our day or help us see the toxic assumptions and the fragile illusions propagated by casual speech, by everyday life, by easier poems.

The Latin poet Horace said that poems ought to *aut prodesse . . . aut delectare*, to delight or instruct. Some poems—easy or hard, direct or indirect—definitely instruct us: they tell us how to live in a certain way, to serve God or treat children gently or start or prevent revolutions, and the techniques of poetry are their means of instruction. At best, such poems embody not just ideas or advice or arguments but wisdom. Chapter 5 shows how *wisdom*, practical or spiritual, gracefully or forcefully delivered, can give you good reasons to care for some poems, from biblical antiquity to our own day.

You can mean you, one person, or a lot of people at once; *we* can mean "you and me," or "you and me and the rest of greater Boston," or "all of us humans." Poems can invoke all these senses of *we* and *you*, all these ways to bring imagined—and real—readers together, in our minds and occasionally in the streets: in other words, they can address or create collectives, communities. We will see how poems speak to the shared lives and the shared language in particular communities, nations, or identity groups. We will also see how some poems, some poets, create communities of our own.

None of these kinds of poems will cure your cough, nor will they abolish capitalism, handle bedtime for a cranky toddler, or free detained refugees. They might, though, help you think about how it would feel to do those things. And they might also introduce you to distinctive characters, subcultures, and ways of life, dazzle you with verbal mastery, challenge the ways in which you interpret the world, connect you to the past, or show how you are not alone.

"I hate classical music," writes Alex Ross, a wonderful, successful critic of classical music; he adds, "Not the thing, but the name." "Poetry" may now have similar problems; it is not only too uniform but too prestigious, too old, and too white. The poet and novelist Ben Lerner wrote a short book called *The Hatred of Poetry* arguing (if I understood him correctly) that poetry, almost by definition, fails (and that we hate it because it fails), since it makes a promise that it cannot keep: to solve the existential problems of isolation, disappointment, meaninglessness, and death. Yet reading, or loving, or hating, something called "poetry" is already a failure: it fails to focus on what's great and wildly various about *poems*. Any focus on one model poem, one great poem or great poet or way to read poems, will fail and fall short unless it acknowledges other ways to read and listen and be. "Everybird has a God. Everybird has a compass in its brain," as the twenty-first-century poet Asiya Wadud quips. Not all birds fly to the same home or seek the same food. Lerner's hatred of poetry comes about because people see poetry as one thing, as if all birds were really one bird, and a white bird, too; no wonder non-white readers resist.

Tommy Pico, a Brooklyn-based poet who identifies as a gay Kumeyaay NDN ("Indian") from what is now Southern California, devoted a whole book, called *Nature Poem*, to that resistance, and it is an astonishing, witty read. One page begins:

> I can't write a nature poem bc English is some Stockholm shit, makes me complicit in my tribe's erasure—why shd I give a fuck abt "poetry"? It's a container

> for words like *whilst* and *hither* and *tamp*. It conducts something of *permanent* and *universal* interest. Poems take something like an apple, turn it into the skin, the seeds, and the core.

Pico—whose "throat is full of survivors"—has to make his own poem, or anti-poem, since prior poets and "poetry," especially "nature poetry," cannot speak for him. That resolve, that action of making words new, is also, for Pico, a kind of destruction:

> I wd give a wedgie to a sacred mountain and gladly piss on
>   the grass of the park of poetic form
>   while no one's lookin
>
> I wd stroll into the china shop of grammar and shout *LET'S
>   TRASH THIS DUMP* then gingerly slip out . . .
>
> Get in, loser—we're touring landscapes of the interior.

("Interior" is a pun: both the inner life, the landscape inside you, and the unglamorous, inland American West.)

Few moves are more exciting than Pico's promise to trash the place, to burn it all down and erect, on the ruins, a poetry or anti-poetry of his own. And few promises are more traditional. The French nineteenth-century poet Paul Verlaine promised (in Conrad Aiken's translation) to "take rhetoric, and wring its neck!" Walt Whitman moved to "cross out all those immensely overpaid accounts," to make poetry as American and as wild and as open as he possibly could, to "unscrew the doors themselves from their jambs!" Each radical poet's place in a tradition of breaking free is not a kind of failure but a description of how some poets find artistic—and emotional, and sometimes political—success. Other poets, of course, have little wish to break free; they live in the house where they (figuratively) grew up, and make their magic from what is already there.

If there were one model for this book (really, there are a few) it would be William Empson's 1930 study *Seven Types of Ambiguity*. That volume—breezy and personal, but definitely more academic than mine—looks at a big stack of poems from the British past in order to show how often poems gain their powers from language that carries multiple meanings: puns, hard-to-parse phrases, terms with long histories, and speakers whose psychology stays unclear. It's also a volume whose author organized it according to categories he made up (kinds and degrees of ambiguity), leaving aside chronological progression and sampling both from Shakespeare and from writers then and now obscure. Empson devoted the book not just to his own idea that ambiguity mattered (a new, controversial idea at the time) but to the wider principle that "you must rely on each particular poem to show you the way in which it is trying to be good": there is no substitute for attention at the level of the poem—even though we can, and we sometimes must, sort the poems into categories anyway, to figure out what each poem is trying to do.

If anyone reads this book in 2188—and I'm not betting that anyone will—they will feel that the poetry of 1998 and 2008 and 2018 is vastly overrepresented. That overrepresentation is not a bug but a feature—I want to show you what's happening now. At the same time, I want to turn you on to Shakespeare and Chaucer, to Langston Hughes and to Marianne Moore, to Li Bai or Sappho or Annamayya in translation, to help you assemble your own usable past. You might find yourself recognizing the styles of some poets I like a lot; other poets I bring up more than once, among them John Donne, Terrance Hayes, Lorine Niedecker, Adrienne Rich, Juan Felipe Herrera, A. R. Ammons, and C. D. Wright. I'd love it if reading my book led you to bring home whole books of their poems, and if reading them spurred you to share them, as the prose poet Killarney Clary wanted to share the people in her memory, who behave, for her, like poems: they "come toward me with names I haven't said aloud in years, each one of you faint but completed. . . . And you say 'Here.' You see what I have, what I might need to tell someone else."

When you have finished this book you will know, and (if I've done it right) be glad you have read, many more poems and parts of poems, and more poets, than you did when you first opened it. But you are not going to like all the poets that I like or all the poems I chose for my examples; if you did, you would likely be me. The right poems for you may not make you more like me; they can, however, change you for the better or help you become who are, who you want to be. They will also give you something that you want to hear, to reread, to share with somebody else. "No one listens to poetry," as the modern poet and cult figure Jack Spicer wrote. And yet, Spicer showed us, a line break could change everything—"No / One listens to poetry." This book will give you a chance to be that one.

chapter one

FEELINGS

HERE IS A POEM ABOUT WHY SOME POETS WRITE POEMS and why some people read them. It is "Autobiographia Literaria," by Frank O'Hara, written early in his career:

When I was a child
I played by myself in a
corner of the schoolyard
all alone.

I hated dolls and I
hated games, animals were
not friendly and birds
flew away.

If anyone was looking
for me I hid behind a
tree and cried out "I am
an orphan."

And here I am, the
center of all beauty!
writing these poems!
Imagine!

"These poems" includes the poem we have just read. Were you sad or antisocial or hard to handle as a child, ever? Are most children antisocial at times? You might look back on those years with good humor or misery, or a little of both. And you might want to see somebody else represent them, so that you feel better understood or less alone. O'Hara mocks the idea that poetry could save your life, that putting painful feelings into words could turn a sad, lonely child into a happy adult. At the same time he seems to feel that it's true, not only for him but maybe for you. O'Hara's word choice seems pedestrian, his line breaks anticlimactic. He even breaks on "a" or "the" three times. And yet, like an airplane pulling out of a nose dive, O'Hara steers the poem toward the humor, the joy, that he shares.

That kind of sharing or vicarious emotion can come to us through a poem, not just through what a poem says but through how, in what shape, with what sounds it says so. Such sharing, such framing, of attitudes and emotions becomes a major goal for many poets, and a good reason to read many poems. I look first at a short poem from Roman antiquity that has survived into the present and then at poems about disparate situations, among them protective parental love, relief after crushing sadness, and the feeling that nobody understands you, that you are your own new kind of hot mess.

Poems that put feeling first are often called lyric poems: they involve a kind of writing, or a way of reading, that treats the poem as a way to embody emotion, almost as if it were sung (and some are also sung). Each of the examples in this chapter says something useful about that category, about lyric poems. I look at how some lyric poems imagine their origins, how poems ask why human beings do something as bizarre as putting our deepest emotions into words. Some of those origin stories are myths (about the semidivine Greek poet Orpheus, for example) and others are metaphors (about bodies and prisons). I look at older poems about the persistence of similar feelings (and symbols, like prisons) through historical time and across international space. I look, also, at older poems—John Donne's in particular—about forms of love that are hard for people who haven't experienced them to understand. And I look at an even older poet who asks what changes when words about feelings are sung.

•

Just as literal songs convey—or intensify, or complicate—the feelings in their words by embedding those words in melodies, vocal delivery, and instrumental arrangements, lyric poems (some of which can also be sung) present, or complicate, or sometimes undermine, the feeling that their words imply, by using patterns of sounds, of syntax, of word choice, of line shapes or references or images. Does the poet use highfalutin vocabulary or low-prestige slang? Do line breaks match the ends of phrases or violate them (as when O'Hara breaks on "the")? What do descriptions tell us about the describer? Can you put yourself in their shoes? How do all these facts about the shape of the poem affect how we feel when we hear it and how its imagined speaker seems to feel?

You can pose these questions to a brand-new poem or to one a few thousand years old, such as this two-line poem by the ancient Roman poet Gaius Valerius Catullus: "Odi et amo. Quare id faciam, fortasse requiris? / Nescio, sed fierei sentio et excrucior." Probably hundreds of writers have put the poem into English (tens of thousands, if you count students in schools); the contemporary poet Frank Bidart has done so three times. One of Bidart's versions reads: "I hate and love. Ignorant fish, who even / wants the fly while writhing." Another: "What I hate I love. Ask the crucified hand that holds / the nail that now is driven into itself, why." There are no fish in the Latin, but there is a cross: a boringly literal version would be something like, "I hate and love. How does that happen, you might ask? / I don't know. But I feel it, and it hurts, like being crucified."

You do not have everything in common with Catullus. For one thing, you are not a citizen of ancient Rome. But you may have something in common with him—and more than you thought before reading the poem. And Catullus's two-line outcry is just one relatively well-known example of a larger phenomenon: very old, very short poems that have survived to produce multiple powerful versions in contemporary English. I could have picked Li Bai, or Sappho, or the Telugu-language *bhakti* poets of South India (try the versions by A. K. Ramanujan). These poems have survived and appeal to later poets as well as to readers not just because they're part of history (what isn't part of history?) but because they are verbal models for the feelings they represent, and some of those feelings appear to have survived. You may have harbored such violently mixed emotions as Catullus's once or twice yourself.

And making small models of complicated feelings, making them out of words and nothing else—making them so that they just might last longer than any one moment, or any one lifetime—is one of the things that poems do especially well. Not all poems do it. Some poems are better when read for the stories they tell, or for their magical obscurity, or for their direct, wise advice. But models of shared or partially shared feelings—models of poems as lyrics—are what a lot of us seek in a lot of new poems, as well as in poems even older than Catullus, even in poems that do everything less directly, through hints or symbols rather than telling us outright (as O'Hara and Bidart do) how someone may feel.

Because lyric poems share feelings using nothing but words, they can—once you get used to reading them, and especially once you get used to old ones—seem to communicate feeling across time and space. We can imagine that we feel at least approximately as Catullus felt, although we can never know for sure, and we can enter that imagination because of the way that Catullus, or Sappho, or Aphra Behn used words. In this case, Bidart's modern translations help (notice how much they differ one from another, too). When you read older lyric poems in English, you are doing the "translation" yourself; it gets easier the more, and the longer, you try. Lyric poetry does not just say that one person felt this way; it puts feelings into words so that other people can enter their arrangements elsewhere, across time and space. And if you read lyric poems from different authors and different periods about the same situation, the same set of feelings, you can sharpen your sense of how style matters, how nuances of language affect the way that emotions get conveyed or reproduced.

Those nuances are why some of us bother with poems, or at least with the poems we call lyric, in the first place, and they become easier to describe the more you attend to multiple times and multiple places (ideally, times and places far beyond the limited, mostly English-language scope of this book).

Some poems try to be lyric—to share feelings, to arrange sets of words so that they reflect emotions—and do it badly; some can be read as lyric if you insist. In the same way, you can use a butter knife or a car key as a screwdriver, but you'll probably get better results if you find a screwdriver for screws and save the car keys for the car. And when you read lyrics, you are, in a sense, finding someone's keys; you may feel that you are opening up a space, or a vehicle, that the poet has occupied so that you can see inside. There's likely some reason the feelings belong in a poem rather than, say, in a telephone call. They might be hard to articulate, or complicated, or shameful, or just so intense that they demand to be shared, as in Laura Kasischke's "Please":

Stay in this world with me.

There go the ships.
The little buses.
The sanctity, the subway.
But let us stay.

Every world has pain,
I knew it when I brought you

to this one. It's true—
the rain is never stopped
by the children's parade. Still

I tell you, it weakens
you after a while into love.

The plastic cow, the plastic barn,
The fat yellow pencil, the smell of paste.

Oh, I knew it wasn't perfect
all along.
Its tears and gravities.
Its spaces and caves.
As I know it again today

crossing the street
your hand in mine
heads bowed in a driving rain.

Spoken first of all to her young child—imagine it said
slowly, with long pauses after line breaks—Kasischke's poem
also includes her hopes for herself. Its direct invitations (beginning with "stay") all have multiple meanings (both "hold
my hand while we cross the street" and "please don't let
anything bad happen to you"). The concessive "still" and "I
know" let her agree that life in "this world" is worthwhile
while acknowledging doubts. Kasischke's few, stray, surprising longer words, like "sanctity" and "gravities"—words few
preschoolers would know—say more about how she regards
this experience, how hard she fears it might be just to help
yourself survive.

Kasischke, like all poets who write lyric poetry, seems to
write both for herself and for imagined readers, about whom
the poet has to make assumptions: that we know plastic toys,
paste, and fat pencils belong with a young child or in a young

child's classroom; that children have to learn to cross the street; that parents belong with children, unless and until they trust someone else (a preschool teacher, for example) with their kids. To read Kasischke's poem sympathetically is to enter into the feelings of the parent, apologizing to her child for this imperfect and unpredictable world.

And that is how lyric poetry works more generally. To read these poems is, in part, or at least temporarily, to share an attitude with the people inside them. Some of these people might as well be the authors behind the poems (if we had to name them, we'd call them "Catullus" or "Laura"). Some are no more—though no less—real than Hermione Granger. But lyric poetry (unlike Hermione) comes to us without a whole story; the imaginary participants in a lyric poem don't have a string of events that cause one another or a satisfying plot behind them, except in a general, conjectural sense. How and when did Catullus's lover refuse him? What street did Kasischke cross? From the poems alone, we cannot begin to say.

This absence of story, or vagueness of story, is for lyric poems a feature, not a bug; lyric poetry can present states of mind, ways to be alive, without having to say how we got there or what happens next. "If you don't have a story, you can still have a style," remarks the poet and critic Jeff Dolven. Lyric poetry lets you show how you feel and share who you might be without having to tell a whole story, as well as inviting you to put yourself in the poet's place. And you can accept that invitation even if you do not, and could not, hold the poet's beliefs or live anything like their life. George Herbert, who died in 1633, became famous afterward for his

Church of England piety; he also wrote prose about how to be a good cleric. Yet anyone of any religion, or none, who has ever recovered from serious mental or physical illness might notice this zigzagging sentence from Herbert's "The Flower":

> And now in age I bud again,
> After so many deaths I live and write;
> I once more smell the dew and rain,
> And relish versing: O my onely light,
> It cannot be
> That I am he
> On whom thy tempests fell all night.

He feels new, though he knows he is the same. The rest of the poem attributes this arc to divine intervention, since Herbert gives thanks for all blessings to God ("onely" is not a typographical error but a now-nonstandard spelling: Herbert's only light is the three-in-one, unified Christian God). You may direct your own gratitude elsewhere and yet inhabit the refreshment, the sweetness, that the poem—with its inwoven rhymes, its celebratory conclusion, its breathtaking "once more"—describes.

If lyric poems embody hard-to-articulate, hard-to-share feelings, making those feelings available through language, then are lyric poems really just therapy? Is reading—or writing—a poem just like seeing a shrink? Particular twentieth-century poets thought so; we will see some of those poets in chapter 2. One of my favorite poets, Randall Jarrell, believed that readers should listen to poems with the same attitude that Freudian psychotherapists bring to their patients: free-floating, undirected, ready for anything. Jarrell wasn't wrong.

But lyric poetry is far older than psychotherapy, and it is never exactly like it (it is also far older than the English language, and older than the words we now use to describe it). Nor is it quite like a conversation with a friend. Lyric poems imagine that they might be spoken to everyone, or to no one, or to a set of strangers, or at least (even when they address friends, as some do) that they might be also be heard and read, much later, by people the poet will never meet. And valuable lyric poems (unlike, say, most transcriptions of phone conversations) reveal new pleasures upon rereading, not just from what they say but from their sounds; they feel at once like expressions and like made things. Morgan Parker, in her 2016 collection *There Are More Beautiful Things Than Beyoncé*, writes tersely and beautifully and (I think) humorously about how poems do what therapists cannot:

> My therapist says something
> in my core is dark and the surface of my planet too
>
> She says *Many creative people*
> & I can't see a beautiful day if I tried
>
> She says peace is something
> people tell themselves

Parker's "core" may resemble the uninhabitable surface of Venus, whose cloudy atmosphere lets very little light through. Her attitude toward her own melancholy is "dark," less about problem-solving, and possibly more realistic, than the advice her therapist can give.

Parker's lines do not sound much like older poems. She seems to go out of her way not to sound like the poems many of us have studied in school. But some of those earlier poets went out of their way not to sound like the poets *they* studied in school, or like the poets they read when young. Reading or writing lyric poems can link us to the distant past (say, to Catullus), but it can also establish us as members of our generation. And Parker herself addresses the feeling that older, more authoritative poems cannot understand how we live now. They sound out of touch, elevated and remote, like obtuse voices from the sky. Or, as Parker put it:

> The fucking sky
> It's so overused because no one's sure of it
> How it floats with flagrant privilege
> And feels it can ask any question
> Everyday its ego gets bigger and you let that happen

Parker will use language that feels as down-to-earth, as unlike skyborne "poetry," as she can make it. The same poem goes on:

> One day your shit will be unbelievably together. . . .
> A gloss will snowfall onto your cheeks, the top of your lip
> The sidewalks will be the same, evidenced
> Combing your records you'll see the past and you'll think OK
> Once I was a different kind of person

The poem embodies not just the mess of Parker's emotions right now but the perfect model of composure that she will be at some time in the future, when other people will look up to her. Her poem gives us the chance not just to inhabit a feeling but to imagine how that feeling can change.

Parker and others write to resist—to attack—older, more dignified tones, as if they want us to feel rather than to get lost in intellection. But intellection helps some of us feel. Readers have feared for centuries that once we take poems apart in order to study them, we will lose our connection to the live feelings inside them; as Wordsworth put it, poetry critics "murder to dissect."There are poems, and pop songs and novels and comic books, that I no longer enjoy because I know too much about how they work or recognize stereotypes on which they depend. But usually, when something is meaningful to me—whether it's a poem, or a song, or a recipe, or a move in basketball—I like it more once I understand more of it. The modern poet and critic William Empson answered similar objections in 1930: "The reasons that make a line of verse likely to give pleasure," he muses, "are like the reasons for anything else; one can reason about them; and while it may be true that the roots of beauty ought not to be violated, it seems to me very arrogant of the appreciative critic to think that he could do this, if he chose, by a little scratching."You can't suck the life out of Herbert's flower by staring at it, even if you try.

I have been mixing old poems with very new ones because I like them both, but also to make a point: to read lyric poetry is to discover commonalities of human feeling—however approximate, however conjectural—across time and space. A. E. Housman's 1896 collection of poems, *A Shropshire Lad*, extraordinarily popular for decades, portrayed mopey, lovelorn young men amid the dales and swales of a stylized rural England. One of those young men mused that some Roman soldier stationed in Britain must have felt much as he did:

Then, 'twas before my time, the Roman
    At yonder heaving hill would stare:
The blood that warms an English yeoman,
    The thoughts that hurt him, they were there.

There, like the wind through woods in riot,
    Through him the gale of life blew high;
The tree of man was never quiet:
    Then 'twas the Roman, now 'tis I.

Now 'tis Morgan Parker, who does not sound much like Housman—but Housman (though he was also a classical scholar) did not sound much like Theocritus, nor like Shakespeare. The long history of lyric poems—even within a single language, like English—shows how much we have in common, in our deepest souls, with the people from long ago, and how those poems promise to convey those commonalities from there and then all the way over to now and here.

You can find such promises—not so distant from Parker's—at the end of John Donne's best poems about misunderstood lovers, probably written in the early 1600s. Right now (those lovers may say) we have only each other. The readers of the future, however, will worship us, praying to us, as saints of love. Donne's poem "The Canonization" ends as those future readers address the lovers, who died long ago:

    "You, whom reverend love
  Made one another's hermitage;
You, to whom love was peace, that now is rage;
    Who did the whole world's soul contract, and drove
      Into the glasses of your eyes

> (So made such mirrors, and such spies,
> That they did all to you epitomize)
> Countries, towns, courts: beg from above
> A pattern of your love!"

A hermitage is a retreat where a hermit could live; "reverend" means "revered." To epitomize is to make an epitome, both a short summary and a best example. The lovers' eyes are their only good mirrors ("glasses") right now; in them, the lovers see only each other. But the future will learn to see, and copy, them too.

Donne is no random example for older lyric poetry, though another critic might give other examples. I bring him up here (we'll see more of him below), not just because I love so much of his work, but because he shows how convoluted, challenging, or apparently antiquated poetic devices—his ultralong sentences, his extended or far-fetched comparisons, his constant hyperbole—can give power and visibility to emotions that would otherwise be hard to express. He shows not just how poems condense and convey feelings but why some emotions are best conveyed in poems, even in convoluted poems, and why it's worth getting used to reading old ones. (Empson defended poems like this one as sincere, against other critics who thought Donne was just showing off: the seventeenth-century poet saw himself, Empson wrote, "as a martyr to love and thereby the founder of a religion" whose doctrine he had to set out.)

Both Donne and Parker compare their poems to mirrors, in which they—and we—might see ourselves; both understand that they might be misunderstood, as Donne has been.

His love poems during much of the twentieth century became famous for their intellectual challenge (they can be hard to understand). But they also represent a deep, rare, even inexplicable intimacy (a connection between two people that nobody else can fully understand).

No poem represents that rare pairing better than "A Valediction Forbidding Mourning." Like all Donne's love poems, it was copied and exchanged and admired in handwritten collections during his lifetime but saw print only after his death. "Valediction" is a Latinate term for "goodbye"; "A Valediction Forbidding Mourning" anticipates a dangerous sea journey like those that, as a sailor and later a diplomat, Donne undertook. Its speaker shows his lover (who may be his wife) that they cannot be defeated by geographic distance because they are always one in the spiritual realm:

> Dull sublunary lovers' love
> (Whose soul is sense) cannot admit
> Absence, because it doth remove
> Those things which elemented it.
>
> But we by a love so much refined,
> That our selves know not what it is,
> Inter-assured of the mind,
> Care less, eyes, lips, and hands to miss.

"Sense" here means something like "physical sensation" or even "lust"; "elemented" means "made up," "composed." The lovers do not themselves have terms for the kind of love that they have, which does not depend on "sense." They will therefore have to create their own terms, by using similes.

Their connection is "like gold to airy thinness beat": gold, unlike more brittle, less valuable metals, can be pounded into smooth, thin sheets. They are also like the legs of a draughtsman's compass:

If they be two, they are two so
　　As stiff twin compasses are two;
Thy soul, the fixed foot, makes no show
　　To move, but doth, if the other do.

And though it in the center sit,
　　Yet when the other far doth roam,
It leans and hearkens after it,
　　And grows erect, as that comes home.

Such wilt thou be to me, who must,
　　Like th' other foot, obliquely run;
Thy firmness makes my circle just,
　　And makes me end where I begun.

Each lover "leans and hearkens" after the other, as if Donne and his intimate friend, lover, or wife heard each other across the sea. The balanced eight-syllable lines, with their alternating rhymes, depend on each other too. Their closure seems "just" both mathematically and morally; in their mutual response, one or both of the lovers stands up, or becomes "erect" (yes, it's a penis joke).

The eighteenth-century critic Samuel Johnson, who wanted his poems deeply felt and sternly clear, disparaged Donne's metaphors as too weird to be true, "heterogenous ideas yoked by violence together." T. S. Eliot and his allies, early in the twentieth century, admired Donne for being weird and difficult, thereby connecting feeling and thinking, mind and heart. As a result of this highbrow history, Donne became a byword for academic, cerebral, disembodied taste; in Margaret Edson's Pulitzer Prize–winning play *Wit* (1999), a repressed college professor pushes Donne on her students as a way to avoid the real heartache in Shakespeare.

And yet. If you yourself have ever felt unique, or confused, or confusing to others, especially in matters of the heart; if you have ever felt that your connection to somebody else— whether or not it is romantic, or exclusive, or recognized by the law—requires some explanation or deserves a passionate defense; if you have friends in a stubborn long-distance relationship; if you have been in any such situation, you might see Donne's elaborate, challenging metaphors not as barriers to sincerity but as ways to achieve it, ways that take advantage of the tools—metaphor, indirection, complex syntax, rhythm—that we can find in poems. You might even, at least if you are looking for them, see in Donne's great love poems, this one among them, defenses of what we now call queer relationships, relationships not sanctioned by custom or law, relationships most people in your own society can't quite understand.

To judge by his own writings about Donne and others, Empson himself—bisexual, polyamorous, and attentive to the lives of people unlike him—saw Donne in just that way: and so, if you want—if you find the right poems—can you. If you are looking for a seventeenth-century woman poet who wrote clear, elegant poems about deep affection between women, you should certainly check out Katherine Phillips. The past wasn't just like the present, but it was closer than many people think; lyric poems can furnish good evidence for both the distance and the closeness.

Lyric poems, even when (like O'Hara's) they are also funny, treat somebody's feelings—yours, mine, anybody's—as worth serious attention. Is that a mistake? The contemporary writer Daphne Gottlieb, known for her spoken-word performances with the early 2000s collective Sister Spit, asks what makes poets important, or self-important, in her own poem "at the punk lit reading." I give the first fifteen lines:

> There is a poet onstage.
> He used to sort of stalk me.
> I clapped at his poem
> because it was over.
> It was about heroin
> or ripping someone off
> or being in a band
> or dead bodies.
> Doesn't everybody want
> to make a statement?
>
> I'm too bored to burn
> down the forest. See the trees?
> Let's bang our heads
> against them until
>
> we see stars.

Gottlieb is not only joking about the clichés she has just heard. She's also asking how much she or you, as writers and listeners, might share this punk-rock dude's all-too-high regard for his own feelings, and how we might take our troubles seriously without sounding like him.

As in literally every lyric poem worth your time, the sound patterns have something to do with the feeling. Gottlieb's suggestions come in three-beat lines (I'M too BORED to BURN / down the FOR-est. SEE the TREES?) whose monosyllables suggest her impatience. But those sound patterns don't always suggest that state of mind. The same rhythm (loose trimeter) that helps Gottlieb sound twitchy and fed-up lets another poet, Stanley Kunitz, come off as deliberate and grave. Here is part of Kunitz's "Hornworm: Summer Reverie":

> See me put on that look
> of slow and fierce surprise
> when I lift my bulbous head
> and glare at an intruder.
> Nobody seems to guess
> how gentle I really am,
> content most of the time
> simply to disappear.

Kunitz—who wrote all his best poems after he turned seventy—made this rough meter his signature, using it not only for his arthropod alter egos but for his other poems about eros and companionship in old age, such as the earnest, winning "Touch Me," which ends:

> So let the battered old willow
> thrash against the windowpanes
> and the house timbers creak.
> Darling, do you remember
> the man you married? Touch me,
> remind me who I am.

Kunitz, like many a pop singer, wants to show that his love is deep and real. Lyric poetry can do that, not just for erotic love but for parental love (as in Kasischke) and for chaste close friends. But lyric poems need not always simply intensify or affirm the emotions they carry. They can also question those emotions, reframe them, attack them, take them apart. For every famous, beautiful, or resonant lyric poem that reinforces stereotypes about sex and love, for example, we can find one whose patterns and arguments undermine those stereotypes instead. You can find both the stereotypes and alternatives to those stereotypes in Donne's body of work: it depends on which poems you read and how you read them. You can find both, too, in Shakespeare. Take his Sonnet 116, which some-times—unfortunately—gets read at weddings:

Let me not to the marriage of true minds
Admit impediments. Love is not love
Which alters when it alteration finds,
Or bends with the remover to remove.
O no! it is an ever-fixed mark
That looks on tempests and is never shaken;
It is the star to every wand'ring bark,
Whose worth's unknown, although his height be taken.
Love's not Time's fool, though rosy lips and cheeks
Within his bending sickle's compass come;
Love alters not with his brief hours and weeks,
But bears it out even to the edge of doom.
    If this be error and upon me prov'd,
    I never writ, nor no man ever lov'd.

If you know anyone who has been dating for more than five weeks, or stayed married for more than five hours, and liked it, then you know people who realize that no minds meet absolutely in every respect, that—as the sex columnist and memoirist Dan Savage put it—"there is no settling down without some settling for." The critic and scholar Helen Vendler, whose ideas about lyric poetry in general I have been echoing, has explained that this sonnet looks like a definition but sounds like a repudiation: "There are too many *no*'s and *nor*'s, *never*'s and *not*'s" for it to be anything else. You can almost hear Shakespeare trying out somebody else's notion of love and deciding that it can't be true: "Love is not love / Which alters when it alteration finds / Nor bends with the remover to remove." Everyone alters, everyone changes with time; if true love requires that nothing and no one change, it follows that true love does not exist, which is the sort of thing you might try to believe if, say, you just caught your ex-lover in a big lie.

"If this be error and upon me prov'd," Shakespeare's concluding couplet spits, "I never writ, nor no man ever lov'd." The test of a couple is not whether they find impediments but whether they overcome them, not whether they fight but how they make up. Shakespeare's comedies depict this kind of erotic love, too, most clearly in Beatrice and Benedick from *Much Ado About Nothing*. You can—if you try hard enough— read Sonnet 116 as another such depiction (love is and must be constant, even when lovers change). But its tone and its word choice and its governing metaphors suggest instead that love only works when lovers themselves do not "alter": that a real lover must not change their feelings, ever, at all. Such a love (as Vendler suggests) is like a star that cannot abide time on Earth; it will not "bend"—and is guaranteed to break. (If you are looking for a Shakespeare sonnet to read at a wedding, try the lovely and unironic Sonnet 18.)

Lyric poems stand out in ways that do not need a story, but you can tell a story around the moments—the child's holding a parent's hand in Kasischke, say— that the poems depict. You can sort these poems out by their situation, their occasion, or by what kinds of speech or writing they mimic or contain: proposal, promise, definition, refutation, answer, confession, fond memory; a funeral song, a description of a cherished object, a landscape, a cityscape. Some kinds of poems have special lit-crit names: aubade (spoken at dawn, often by lovers parting), prothalamion (to be read before a wedding). Some poets string lyric poem after lyric poem together until they appear to tell a longer story: Renaissance poets did it with sets of sonnets, though no one knows whether Shakespeare intended the order in which his own sonnets appeared.

You can also find lyric poems stuck, like the fruit in fruitcakes, inside other kinds of long stories, in modern novels and in medieval narrative verse. One of my favorite very old lyric poems pops up inside "The Franklin's Tale," the most beautiful and most underrated of Geoffrey Chaucer's *Canterbury Tales*. In it, the faithful wife Dorigen has been waiting for her husband Arviragus to come back from overseas. He's late: Has he abandoned her? No, she decides; he has more likely died at sea. She puts her fears for him into a passionate denunciation of the rocks that endanger ships on the Breton coast, which (she suspects) have wrecked the ship that carried him. I give the lines first in their Middle English spelling, so that you can hear the sounds they make—please do try reading them out loud; my modern translation follows after that.

> Than wolde she sitte adoun upon the grene,
> And pitously into the see biholde,
> And seyn right thus, with sorweful sikes colde:
> Eterne god, that thurgh thy purveyaunce
> Ledest the world by certein governaunce,
> In ydel, as men seyn, ye no thyng make,
> But, lord, thise grisly feendly rokkes blake,
> That semen rather a foul confusion
> Of werk than any fair creacion
> Of swich a parfit wys God and a stable
> Why han ye wroght this werk unresonable?

> Then she would sit down upon the green
> And piteously look into the sea,
> And say right then, with sorrowful, cold sighs:
> Eternal God, who through your prearrangement
> Lead the world and are its government,
> You make nothing—men say—idly, without a reason.
> And yet these grisly, devilish black rocks
> That seem more like a foul confusion
> Than any fair or beautiful creation
> Of such a perfect God, so wise and stable:
> Why did you make them so unreasonable?

It is one of the earliest such laments in English. Why would a good God make this terrible sea with its black rocks that (Dorigen believes) have probably shipwrecked her true love? The narrative stops for her expostulation, as if to invite her listeners to join in. In fact, Arviragus is fine—he eventually comes home—but while he's gone, the unscrupulous Aurelius, who has fallen in love (he calls it love) with Dorigen, tries to seduce her. While Dorigen pines, Aurelius makes up poems about her, using fashionable French verse forms:

> He was despeyred; no thyng dorste he seye,
> Save in his songes somwhat wolde he wreye
> His wo, as in a general compleynyng;
> He seyde he lovede and was biloved no thyng.
> Of swich matere made he manye layes,
> Songes, compleintes, roundels, virelayes,
> How that he dorste nat his sorwe telle,
> But langwissheth as a furye dooth in helle.

> He was in despair. He dared say nothing
> Except in his songs, where he would reveal
> His woes, making his complaint general:
> He said he loved but nobody loved him.
> He made many poems from such material:
> Songs, complaints, roundels, and virelays,
> About his sorrow that he dared not tell,
> But languished, as a fury does in Hell.

Chaucer does not give us the words to Aurelius's virelays or roundels: the poet prefers that he tell us about Aurelius but that we overhear, and feel for, Dorigen.

I loaded this chapter with love poems because so many of us first encounter serious lyric poetry that way, and because most of us have felt something like romantic or erotic attachment, though of course not everyone does: some poets with rich emotional lives might today be called asexual or aromantic, among them my favorite modernist, Marianne Moore. I chose poems of love and attachment (not, say, grief or rage) for an introduction to lyric poetry, too, because the intimate connection that these poems envision, or seek, between an "I" and a "you," in soul or body, resembles the intimate connection that lyric poems seek between poet and reader, a figurative meeting of the minds.

And yet there are other ways to tell the story of what lyric poetry is and how it arose. For Abdelfattah Kilito, an expert on Arabic poetry, "lamentations for the dead are at the origins of poetry. The primordial poetic genre, the one from which all others derive, is the elegy." The first great lyric in Near Eastern antiquity is also a poem of mourning, the hero's lament for his friend-lover-companion Enkidu, in the Sumerian *Epic of Gilgamesh*. Here is the start of tablet 8, in David Ferry's 1992 translation:

With the first light of the early morning dawning,
in the presence of the old men of the city,

Gilgamesh, weeping, mourned for Enkidu:
"It is Enkidu, the companion, whom I weep for,

weeping for him as if I were a woman.
He was the festal garment of the feast.

On the dangerous errand, in the confusions of noises,
he was the shield that went before in the battle;

he was the weapon at hand to attack and defend.
A demon has come and taken away the companion.

He ranged the hills together with the creatures
whose hearts delight to visit the watering places.

A demon has come and taken him away."

Here is a template for so many later kinds of lyric complaint: the poem as a way to push back against an unjust world, a world that insists on taking away what—or, worse, who—we love. Here, too, are common rhetorical and technical moves of later lyric poems: simile (saying that something is like something else); metaphor (saying that something *is* something else); repetition (as if to defeat the passage of time); and the appearance of solitude. This mourner seems to be talking past his actual hearers, singing or complaining to himself and repeating what he cannot believe. Compulsive repetition recurs in later poems of loss and grief: Federico García Lorca's great multipart *llanto* (lament) for the bullfighter Ignacio Sánchez Mejías repeats Sánchez Mejías's time of death ("a las cinco de la tarde," five in the afternoon) twenty-eight times.

Love poems and laments are joined at the root, since both are ordinarily about wanting something or someone you cannot have, speaking to or about someone you cannot touch or see, at least not yet, or not here, or not now. (Nobody writes a love poem while kissing, though you could write one while holding hands.) You could say that common element makes poems of romantic love or poems of grief the truest examples, the sources of all other lyric poems. You could also say instead that there is no single true source of song, no single emotion more basic than all the others, no more than there is one source for every river: there is only a wide array of human emotions and an even broader array of ways to put them into words. Even if that's what you think (and it's what I think), you might take an interest in myths and stories about the source of lyric poetry: about why we need it and why it arose.

In the most famous Western myth on that subject, the not-quite-divine musician Orpheus sang so beautifully that he persuaded the god of the underworld to let him bring his late wife back from the dead, then lost her when he turned around to look at her on her way back to life. That myth proposes that lyric poetry is at base erotic, about attachment; that it is first and last about grief or lack or loss; that it feels magical, that it can contradict facts (for example, the fact that death is forever); and, maybe, that it is really about itself—true poets might not so much sing about their love as love in order to sing. The first sonnet in Terrance Hayes's *American Sonnets for My Past and Future Assassin* concludes in an anecdote about Orpheus:

> Orpheus was alone when he invented writing.
> His manic drawing became a kind of writing when he sent
> His beloved a sketch of an eye with an X struck through it.
> He meant *I am blind without you.* She thought he meant
> *I never want to see you again.* It is possible he meant that too.

Does he want his beloved back? Or does he want to write poems? That *X*, that crossed-out eye, that visible sign of blindness, that letter that could be a number or an algebraic variable, reflects a severe division, a poet who wants mutually exclusive things. A later sonnet decides that "Eurydice is actually the poet, not Orpheus. Her muse / Has his back to her with his ear bent to his own heart."

Orpheus is—whatever he intends—in the end unhappy. Yet lyric poems, poems that embody and try to share feeling, are not only versions of unhappiness or complaints; they are also promises, celebrations, ways to tease and to give new hope. The most durable lyric poems—the ones that provoke imitation as well as discussion over years or centuries—need not be happy or sad, but they tend to be passionately complicated. Catullus recorded his hate along with his love. The ancient Greek poet Sappho calls love *glukupikron,* "sweet-bitter" (normally translated "bittersweet"), and the poet and classical scholar Anne Carson has unfolded a whole theory of love, and love poetry, from the contradictions in that one Greek word. Emily Dickinson also reveled in her own escape from easy decoding: "I dwell in Possibility," one poem begins, "a fairer House than Prose."

Lyric poetry can seem direct ("I hate and love") or indirect (thirty-six lines of landscape description, say, from which emotions may be inferred). It may seem careful and tentative, or exuberant, or grim, or bold. What it always does, by definition, is give a sense of feeling put into words. The lyric poem does not simply express something particular to one speaker, one personality, one poet, oneself. (There are poems that do; we will see them in chapter 2.) Instead it says—distinctively, memorably, often indirectly—what the poet Hera Lindsay Bird, in her long, self-mocking poem "Mirror Traps," says directly: "There is something wrong with you that is also wrong with me."

In looking at herself, in finding a form that suits their own feelings, such a poet also describes, and envisions, the attitudes of their potential readers in a kind of double vision that Bird, with typical nonchalance, compares to a "discount facial peel": "cucumber slices / floating on my eyelids // like a double-salad monocle." Without the metaphors and masks and mirrors, we would not be able to see her soul, or her face. With them, we can feel that she has seen part of us and we have seen a portion of her, in this case an uncomfortable, exasperated, unruly, discomfiting, and also comic portion, not quite what a photograph could show. A poem like Bird's, dependent on its images, nearly tells us what the signs on the sides of buses and trucks tell drivers: IF YOU CAN'T SEE MY MIRRORS I CAN'T SEE YOU. And new kinds of poetry can feel like new kinds of mirrors, as in Brandon Som's "Seascapes":

> A subway car sounds like you
> Searching the silverware
> For a tablespoon, while tunnels turn
> The windows of a train to mirrors
> Because the opaque, in its refusing
> Of the light, affords us reflection.

Som sees himself as a window that works like a mirror; James Merrill, fifty years earlier, portrayed himself as a mirror, speaking to a facing window across a long room:

> I grow old under an intensity
> Of questioning looks. *Nonsense,*
> I try to say. *I cannot teach you children*
> *How to live.—If not you, who will?*
> Cries one of them aloud, grasping my gilded
> Frame till the world sways. *If not you, who will?* . . .
> If ever I feel curious
> As to what others endure,
> Across the parlor *you* provide examples,
> Wide open, sunny, of everything I am
> Not. You embrace a whole world without once caring
> To set it in order. That takes thought.

The lines reflect Merrill's own taste and self-presentation: reflective, with a preference for intricate patterning, like the embedded rhymes ("will"-"gilded," "curious"-"endure," "examples"-"am") that continue through a dozen more couplets. Merrill hides and emerges—shy, observant, elusive, seeking an "order" he has not yet found—almost as those rhymes emerge throughout the poem.

Lyric poems show you yourself *and* somebody else; they show you what you have in common, not with everybody, but with somebody else, which means that they can be mirrors and also windows. W. B. Yeats complained that a poet he liked without loving, the Irish nationalist James Clarence Mangan, "never startles us by saying beautifully things we have long felt. He does not say look at yourself in this mirror; but rather, 'Look at me—I am so strange, so exotic, so different.'" The best lyric poets say both. And poets have compared their own works to mirrors, and to windows, and even to both at once, since long before Som, or Bird, or Merrill, or Yeats. Donne, in "A Valediction: Of My Name in the Window," compared his poem to a pane of glass in which he had scratched his own name. His beloved might therefore see herself and think of him: "Here you see me, and I am you." And that reflection—if you choose to accept it, and not everyone does—is how lyric poems in general work: you see, for a moment, both outside yourself and into yourself.

Of course, you will not see yourself in every lyric poem— sometimes the pleasure in reading lyric poems involves discovering structures of feeling you have never encountered, or never understood. Not every lyric poem seems meant for you. Some poems seem meant for a small group of like-minded souls: "Fit audience find, though few," as John Milton put it. Others aspire to reach us all. Walt Whitman even wrote a poem about that aspiration, called simply "To You":

> Even now your features, joys, speech, house, trade, manners,
>   troubles, follies, costume, crimes, dissipate away from you,
> Your true soul and body appear before me,
> They stand forth out of affairs, out of commerce, shops, work,
>   farms, clothes, the house, buying, selling, eating, drinking,
>   suffering, dying.
>
> Whoever you are, now I place my hand upon you, that
>   you be my poem,
> I whisper with my lips close to your ear,
> I have loved many women and men, but I love none
>   better than you.

The earliest version of that poem, from 1856, carried an even more revealing title: "Poem of You, Whoever You Are."

To read a poem as lyric, once more, is to say how it feels, how the person the poem imagines might feel: angry, sad, happy, surprised, delighted, apprehensive? We can then ask why, and how those feelings change in the course of the poem, and what parts of the language the poem has arranged make those feelings vivid (if they are vivid) for us, how and why they arose. Memorable lyric poems do not just say how somebody feels (which, after all, as O'Hara quipped, you can do by picking up a telephone); they show those feelings, giving them shape and sound, and thereby—at least potentially—preserve them for strangers, for future generations. Lyric poetry connects people to other people by showing (not only stating but showing) what might be hiding in someone else's heart. The contemporary American poet Chen Chen goes so far as to describe his work this way: "My job is to trick adults // into knowing they have / hearts."

No wonder, then, that reading the right poems (the poems that are right for you, or for your heart) can make you want to write them. Both Dorigen and Aurelius, in Chaucer, imitate the then-new poems they have read. The history of any kind of poetry or poetic goal, lyric or otherwise, is a history of imitations. At the same time, that history is also a history of divergence, speciation, and obsolescence, of writers who substitute Beyoncé for basilicas, who give a wedgie to a sacred mountain, who say (it is the half-mocking first line of a poem by John Ashbery) "You can't say it that way any more." You can follow these divergent responses to what are still common human feelings (erotic attachment, grief, loyalty, curiosity) through very broad traditions and widely used forms: the sonnet, say, or the funeral elegy.

You can also follow much narrower traditions, seeing how lyric poetry works across the ages by seeing how it responds to one problem that poets cannot wholly solve. One such chain consists of poems in which spring—renewal, fulfillment, fertility, creative success—has come for other people, but not for the speaker or singer.

> Summer is come, for every spray now springs;
> The hart hath hung his old head on the pale;
> The buck in brake his winter coat he flings;
> The fishes flete with new repairèd scale.

That's Henry Howard, Earl of Surrey, writing probably in the 1640s. He likes what he sees in this sonnet (I give lines 5–8), but the greenness of spring has not reached, and may never reach, his heart: "Each care decays, and yet my sorrow springs." Mary Wroth, about fifty years later, put the same situation into shorter, sadder lines:

The Spring now come at last
    To Trees, Fields, to Flowres,
And Meadowes makes to taste
    His pride, while sad showres
Which from mine eyes doe flow
    Makes knowne with cruell paines,
    Cold Winter yet remaines,
No signe of Spring wee knowe.

Wroth likes spring less, and condemns it more, than Surrey did; the whole project of blossoming and blooming feels, to her, like culpable pride. Samuel Taylor Coleridge, around 1820, picked up the baton:

The bees are stirring—birds are on the wing—
And Winter slumbering in the open air,
Wears on his smiling face a dream of Spring!
And I the while, the sole unbusy thing,
Nor honey make, nor pair, nor build, nor sing.

Coleridge dissociates his fauna and flora from one another; they do not all speak with one voice, nor in parallel lines, nor for the same number of syllables. And yet they still fit together, in an outdoor harmony whose ease excludes him.

These poems also show how description—words for things seen, or heard, or explored—can become, framed rightly, a way to make lyric poems. How you describe a meadow, or a deer, or a sewing machine, says a lot about what you notice and therefore about how you feel. You can find other frustrating or failing springs all over T. S. Eliot's *The Waste Land*: for Eliot, for people who feel left out as he does, for people who still feel dry or infertile or chilly, "April is the cruelest month," as Eliot says in the famous opening line. Fifty-odd years after Eliot, Louise Glück turned her own springtime anxieties into her poem "For Jane Myers":

> Look how the bluet falls apart, mud
> pockets the seed.
> Months, years, then the dull blade of the wind.
> It is spring! We are going to die!
>
> And now April raises up her plaque of flowers
> and the heart
> expands to admit its adversary.

Glück ends her spring poem not so much with humility as with the balance you see at the start of a sporting event between two teams that want to win. Will nature, which tends toward novelty, defeat the heart, which—for Glück—craves certainty and permanence? Glück's wind is not just a knife but a dull one; it's boring, and repetitive, and painful, and it takes too long to cut what it cuts. That one word, "dull," gives one more sharp example of how descriptive choice, in a lyric poem, can open out into feeling.

Lyric poetry is not just a way to give voice to shared or potentially shared feelings; it is also a way to imagine a soul or a self or a voice that reaches beyond one body, one story, one time, one life. No wonder so many poems imagine their speakers becoming something else; no wonder so many imagine living in—or escaping from—some sort of prison or cage. In seventh-century China a poet named Lo Pin-wang felt imprisoned at once by his literal captors and by time and by his advancing age. His response reads, in part, in Stephen Owen's translation:

> How can I bear those shadows of black locks
> That come here to face my "Song of White Hair"?
> Dew heavy on it, can fly no farther toward me;
> The wind strong, its echoes easily lost.

In an analogy that seems to hold across cultures, a lyric poem is the song of a caged bird but also the cry of a figure in prison. Donne's recondite but passionate poem "The Ecstasy" asked "lovers' souls" to "descend" back into their bodies, "else a great prince in prison lies." A generation after Donne, Andrew Marvell imagined a verse dialogue between body and soul, each of which felt imprisoned by the other: "What magic could me thus confine," the soul asked, "within another's grief to pine?" Richard Lovelace, a contemporary of Marvell, wrote by far his most popular poem from the literal prison in which he was thrown after his side (the king's side) lost a war. People today quote the poem without knowing the source: "Stone walls do not a prison make, / Nor iron bars a cage."

To read lyric poetry across the centuries is to see how often we feel alone and confined to our single bodies and lives. Lyric poems become ways to fly, or break out, or tunnel away, as if our one life were a prison or the soul a songbird, beating its wings against a cage (a startlingly common figure for lyric poetry, and one we will see again near the end of this book). But to follow the metaphor of poem as cell, of body as prison, is also to think about poets who have spent time in real prisons, from Lo Pin-wang to Lovelace to poets in our own day. The contemporary American poet Reginald Dwayne Betts, in "Supreme Mathematics," watches men in a prison gym, seeing the failed stoicism in their routines and in his truncated, short-of-breath lines:

> Cold air pushes hard
> out their mouths.
> They count off reps.
> When they pull, the splash
>
> of colors against their skin
> splices the air. Each rep
> could be a year in prison
> and after two hours
>
> Wise would still be
> counting, the sound
> of numbers snuffing
> out everything else.

"Numbers," as Betts must know, once meant "verse" ("I lisped in numbers, for the numbers came," wrote Alexander Pope); "reps" (repetitions) belong to the incarcerated men's exercise routines. Betts's quatrains combine the isolation of prison, the wish for community or communion, and the melancholy pleasures of verse form.

Hayes, in another one of his *American Sonnets*, takes the ideas of body as prison and poetic form as both liberation and confinement further still: the poet, fed up with himself and with his society, tells himself, or part of himself:

> I lock you in an American sonnet that is part prison,
> Part panic closet, a little room in a house set aflame. . . .
> I lock your persona in a dream-inducing sleeper hold. . . .
> I make you a box of darkness with a bird in its heart.

Lyric poetry—the poet imagines—works by finding words for someone's passions, which could also be your own: it can get you out of your one situation, your one body, your one life, though it will not literally free you from a literal jail. It may, though, take up many aspirations to freedom, from the traditions of prison writing to the tradition of existential rebellion against everything that exists, in which the poet wishes they could be a force of nature, like the air or the wind, as in Percy Bysshe Shelley's "Ode to the West Wind":

> If I were a dead leaf thou mightest bear;
> If I were a swift cloud to fly with thee;
> A wave to pant beneath thy power, and share
>
> The impulse of thy strength, only less free
> Than thou, O uncontrollable!

The contemporary poet Magdalena Zurawski describes, in a long poem called "The Remainders," the experience of writing her poems as if she were breaking herself open, and also as if she were breaking free, emphasizing the multiple meanings in the word *break*:

> one night a single word opened to me to repeat itself as if
> I were its instrument I was helpless in its cycle . . .

the weather broke
the bough broke
my voice broke

Poetry, for Zurawski as for Shelley, turns line breaks into ways to escape the body, to break apart the constraints of home and society. She writes, in the same poem: "I saw a door of light and there I entered and took on the light and felt my elsewhere breaking loose and I said to the world . . . business is work done by animals but poetry is something else." When lyric poems sound distinctive, or memorable, or somehow new, we can imagine the poem as a kind of breaking free or breaking away from mere words on the page and into the realm of the spirit, where souls meet souls. That claim sounds like hokum to some; to others, it simply describes what happens when we read our favorite poems.

That escape happens—if it happens—by means of technique: form in poems, arrangements for words and their sounds, work like vocal techniques and chord progressions and instrument timbres in songs. When a poem works as a lyric, it can feel less like mere words and more like a song. And song, more than anything else that human beings can make or do together, seems to express the truth of a life within. As Tracey Thorn has explained, a singer's "unique voice—whether we believe it to be entirely natural, 'authentic,' or at least in part a created or discovered thing—opens up a direct conduit to the soul, or the personality." That's one reason the term *lyric* seems to fit these kinds of poems. Another reason emerges from the history of lyric poems, the history of short poems that resemble songs: if you go back far enough, these poems *were* sung, and the oldest kinds that you cannot easily sing (sonnets, for example) evolved as variations on kinds that you can. As the scholar Marisa Galvez has shown, some kinds of modern lyric poetry probably originated when musicians and scribes at late medieval courts copied down words to songs, then passed on the copies to people who might never hear the tunes. "Lettered men used [the songbooks] to transform their lyrics into . . . a literary tradition comprising what we accept today as 'poets' and 'poetry.'"

By the time that transformation fully hit the English language, in the middle of the sixteenth century, it was mixed up with the advent of movable type and the printing of books. The major lyric poet of this period, just before Shakespeare, was Thomas Wyatt, who wrote many poems that were or might have been sung. One such poem is usually called, after its first line, "My lute, awake." The eight-stanza poem begins:

> My lute, awake! perform the last
> Labor that thou and I shall wast
>   And end that I have now begun;
> For when this song is sung and past,
>   My lute, be still, for I have done.

("Wast," or "waste," rhymes with "last" and "past" in Wyatt's Tudor English.) His lute will wake up in order to be told, immediately, to go back to sleep, and this time for good; when he is done with the song, he will be done ("for I have done") with his sadness, as if the whole song had taken place in a single moment of regret, a moment distinguished also by its braided *s* and *l* sounds and by its stubborn refrain:

As to be heard where ear is none,
As lead to grave in marble stone,
    My song may pierce her heart as soon:
Should we then sigh, or sing, or moan?
    No, no, my lute, for I have done.

The composition will be a "waste" if its only goal is to sway an unresponsive lady. But really the goal is expression: he does not want to persuade her to do anything so much as he wants to escape from his own well of sadness by showing himself, and us, how it feels, in words that resonate in some of our memories long after the song's performance, and Wyatt's era, are done.

That's how a poem can share feelings we imagine the poet—or someone, somewhere—has experienced, feelings you might experience too; that's how poems can be lyric (whether or not they can also be, or refer to, the lyrics and the music in songs). But what if a poem asks us to imagine not just someone's feelings so much as . . . someone? Someone who may be the poet, or may not be the poet, but who isn't just anyone (and who isn't you)? What if we go to a poem (perhaps a lyric poem) looking not for expression, for shared emotion, but for an individual, for a character?

chapter two

CHARACTERS

P OEMS CAN PORTRAY SHARED FEELINGS, STATES OF MIND
that you too may have had, from rueful joy to rageful
grief; they can serve as mirrors, as doors, as cells, as keys
to cells, as songs we learn or know or want to sing. They
can also introduce us to other people. Some poets construct
characters almost as playwrights do: figures speak and behave
almost as if onstage. Other poets turn themselves into recognizable characters, writing up scenes from their own lives or
just exercising their hard-to-imitate style: "Had I met these
lines running wild in the deserts of Arabia," Coleridge wrote
of a favorite sentence, "I should have instantly screamed
out 'Wordsworth'!" Poems and poets who don't make you
scream might delight you anyway as you recognize the individuals behind their phrases and sounds. The first question to
ask when you read poems in this way (when poems seem to
want to be read in this way) is not "How do you feel?" but

"Who seems to be speaking? What are they like, and how do you know?"

This chapter will look at several kinds of poems that focus on characters. Most of those poems will tell you that's what they're doing; some comment on their own goals at length. First we'll see poems that liken themselves to portraits, or to self-portraits, poems that feel very much like recorded speech, and poems that riff on characters' names. We will see poems in which the characters at the core of the poems, or the poets behind them, compare themselves to nonhuman animals, to inanimate objects, to more than one thing at once. We will also look at ambitious modern poems that connect characters to society, who one person is and has been to what other people, and what forces made them that way. We'll see how memorial poems sketch particular characters' whole lives from the outside and after the fact. And we will see a famous kind of poem that presents a particular character, the dramatic monologue, in which we get to listen to characters as if they were speaking aloud, onstage; we overhear them, and they show us who they are.

Lyric poems are like songs, like scores we can learn to sing, or, on occasion, like mirrors; poems of character are like people we could meet, and so it is no wonder that they so often compare themselves to portraits, photographs, paintings. No wonder, then, that so many contemporary poems announce themselves by the title "Self-Portrait." The trend likely began with John Ashbery's famous and uncommonly long *Self-Portrait in a Convex Mirror* (1975). Since then we have had, among many others, Lucie Brock-Broido's "Self-Portrait with Her Hair on Fire" and "Self-Portrait in the Miraculous

World, with Nimbed Ox"; Dean Rader's collection *Self-Portrait as Wikipedia Entry*; Jorie Graham's "Self-Portrait as the Gesture Between Them"; Monica Youn's "Self-Portrait in a Wire Jacket"; and Diane Seuss's "Self-Portrait with the Ashes of My Baby Blanket." Meghan O'Rourke, coming late to the subgenre, contributed "Self-Portrait as Myself." Seuss's collection *Still Life with Two Dead Peacocks and a Girl* has other poems that function like self-portraits, ways in which Seuss assembles her most telling memories. "I Look at My Face in a Red Mylar Balloon Tied to a Mailbox" remembers a birthday party gone wrong, setting Seuss's remembered childhood among other people from her perhaps rough neighborhood:

> Rhonda with the rusty birthmark on her neck who could
> lasso anything
> and Rick playing the blues in his red trailer with his waist-
> length hair
> and Ellie pregnant with his baby, her red belly button turned
> inside out
>
> my beet-colored hair blown over my eyes
> my mouth, bloody as if recently beaten
>
> and when the wind blows the balloon closer, all I am is
> wounded mouth
>
> when I open it I can swallow the town

Beet-red, rust-red, blood-red; the poem reflects a face, but it also reflects (like Stephen King's *Carrie*) pervasive and unspoken trauma, with a character who sees blood colors everywhere. Other poems of self-portraiture give, directly, the poet's imagined face. Rainer Maria Rilke's "Self-Portrait,

1906," in Stephen Mitchell's translation, begins at "the forehead still naïve, / most comfortable in shadows, looking down"; the poet, for all his vagueness and ductility, looks "as though, from far off, with scattered Things, / a serious, true work were being planned." One of Hayes's *American Sonnets* repeats the idea that in lyric poetry, one generation sees another's face: "Sometimes the father almost sees looking / At the son, how handsome he'd be if half / His own face was made of the woman he loved."

And Hayes—a serious amateur painter himself—was hardly the first poet to attend to the practice of painting someone's portrait. The English Victorian poet Christina Rossetti spent her writing life among painters, including her brother Dante Gabriel Rossetti, also a poet, critic, and translator. During the 1850s Dante Gabriel drew and painted, over and over, Elizabeth Siddal, the object of his affections (they later married); in 1856 Christina wrote her careful, ambivalent sonnet "In an Artist's Studio" about Dante's devotion to Elizabeth:

> One face looks out from all his canvases,
> One selfsame figure sits or walks or leans;
> We found her hidden just behind those screens,
> That mirror gave back all her loveliness.
> A queen in opal or in ruby dress,
> A nameless girl in freshest summer greens,
> A saint, an angel—every canvas means
> The same one meaning, neither more nor less.
> He feeds upon her face by day and night,
> And she with true kind eyes looks back on him,
> Fair as the moon and joyful as the light;
> Not wan with waiting, not with sorrow dim;

Not as she is, but was when hope shone bright;
Not as she is, but as she fills his dream.

The painter seeks variety, dressing his model up over and over, but his canvases show a bittersweet unity. He stays devoted to his unchanging idea of her, even as she has grown "wan," or lost hope, under his idolizing gaze; he paints her, but the sonnet paints him. Perhaps afraid to offend her brother, Christina did not publish this sonnet during her lifetime; it first saw print in 1896.

Poems about individual characters may work like portraits, but they also compete with actual portraits: Whose art is better? Whose art can show the truth of who somebody is? Renaissance authors called a competition between different art forms (poetry and painting; sculpture and painting; architecture and sculpture) a *paragone*; you can see it take place in Christina Rossetti's sonnet, which has no "I," no "you," and no compunctions about implying that the poem's arrangements of words can tell us more than any oil or tempera or engraving—and more than any paragraph of prose—about what's going on in these people's heads.

Ben Jonson, one of the first English-language writers to give his own titles to his short poems, entitled one of his quirkiest poems "My Picture Left in Scotland." The poem contains a *paragone* of its own. The title means that he had left a portrait miniature of himself, perhaps a locket, up north with a lady whose company he had enjoyed. But Jonson was famously portly and unattractive. That picture might not so much maintain their connection as discourage her from inviting him back:

I now think Love is rather deaf than blind,
For else it could not be
That she,
Whom I adore so much, should so slight me
And cast my love behind.
I'm sure my language to her was as sweet,
And every close did meet
In sentence of as subtle feet,
As hath the youngest He
That sits in shadow of Apollo's tree.

O, but my conscious fears,
That fly my thoughts between,
Tell me that she hath seen
My hundred of gray hairs,
Told seven and forty years
Read so much waste, as she cannot embrace
My mountain belly and my rocky face;
And all these through her eyes have stopp'd her ears.

Jonson really did have an unusually large belly, although
we might now frown at his intimation that forty-seven is
horribly old. His larger point, though, is more general and
more serious: verse should give a better, more accurate portrait of Ben Jonson, perhaps of anyone, than a visible face
and body can provide. This verse, for example, suggests a
self-deprecating, loquacious man who might make excellent
conversation. And yet this poetic self-portrait, the one in his
words, is mostly a portrait of doubts: we see him reacting to
how he believes she will see him and doubting that she will
love him for what's inside.

Yeats wrote that his stage plays tried to portray "character isolated by a deed": poets can show characters in short poems not so much by telling us how they look but by framing one action they took, one deed. Sometimes—as with "In an Artist's Studio"—the poet tones her own style down, attempts to get out of the way, so that somebody else's character can show through. Other poets find an affinity between their idiosyncratic style and the odd character they want to portray, as in Allan Peterson's "Hitting the Hot Spots" (I give the whole poem):

> Carol who would not hurt the fruit flies heat-stunned
> on the red bedspread under her goose-neck reading lamp
> slipped paper we still call typewriter under two and moved
> them closer to the phone hoping they'd recover.

Carol's admirable but extreme attention to very small, barely alive things matches the similar—even awkward or excessive—attention that Peterson's own language shows for the history of the things he sees, a verbal care (or finickiness) that defines his peculiarities almost as tactile care defines hers. Peterson is a painter too (for most of his adult life he taught painting at a community college in Florida). A similar verbal-and-visual individuality animates another of Peterson's distinctive very short poems, one about fitting in and standing out, called "Vignette":

> There is a heartbreaking earnestness to life
> On the midway a man was selling chameleons
> He had many on strings pinned to his vest
> It was Royal Stewart plaid They were trying

The salesman wants to fit in (to the market economy); he wants to sell chameleons (interchangeable products), which themselves want to fit in (via camouflage), although they can't (there is no way they can blend with that plaid). At the same time, the salesman wants to stand out: these contradictory wishes may be the poet's too.

Other poets show us their characters through the nuances of those characters' speech. In William Carlos Williams's "The Last Words of My English Grandmother" we can hear, or infer, not just the grandmother but also the poet, listening, bending in close, as the cadence speeds up and then suddenly stops. The poem takes place in an ambulance. Near the end,

> we passed a long row
> of elms. She looked at them
> awhile out of
> the ambulance window and said,
>
> What are all those
> fuzzy-looking things out there?
> Trees? Well I'm tired
> of them and rolled her head away.

As usual, Williams's free verse relies on enjambment, that is, on breaks that do not match the ending of a sentence or a phrase. Above all, the poem turns on that last enjambment between "I'm tired" and "of them"; the poem pauses and then restarts so that we can take in her own sense that it's time to go. This woman is "tired," and not just of looking at trees.

Her disdain for her surroundings, her lifelong sense that she should be in charge, and her physical exhaustion all come through in the single concluding gesture, the last of her life, as well as in her last words.

Writers like Williams—famously extroverted, a pediatrician and an ob-gyn during the decades when he wrote most of his poems—fill their work with characters drawn from life. More introverted poets portray few people besides themselves; if you read their work at length you get to know *them.* A. R. Ammons (who published a book every couple of years from the early 1960s until his death in 2002) was one of those introverts. Diffident, shy, prolific, and almost rambling (as in his essay "A Poem Is a Walk"), at home with the quantitative sciences, Ammons and his attitudes seem part and parcel of his ambulatory cadence, whether he is interpreting physical chemistry or taking a walk in the snowy woods of Ithaca, New York, where he spent most of his adult life. His late poem "A Little Thing Like That" concludes with a kind of prayer that is, also, self-portraiture:

> may I wander
> with meanders, not seeing far (ahead
>
> or behind) and picking up willows
> wherever possible, or alders and .
>
> stopping to have lunch in the shade
> and drink from boulder-drained melts.

Ammons, too, enjambs the heck out of his lines, imitating an inconclusive "meander"; the shy wanderings of his sentences (we will see more of them in chapter 5) fit his humbly science-based, almost sheepishly inconclusive view of life.

Juan Felipe Herrera, a very public author (also the last US poet laureate under President Obama), may seem like Ammons's opposite: where Ammons was formed by the sciences, shyness, and snow, Herrera developed his insistently extroverted approach to literary creation out of the Southern California Latinx/Chicanx protest theater of the 1970s. And yet he makes an equally good example of a poet with an instantly recognizable, hard-to-imitate style. We recognize Herrera by the speed with which he moves between exclamations, by his density of proper nouns, by his digressive verbal heterogeneity, and by the many kinds of people (some of them almost always vulnerable: children, immigrants, the historically dispossessed) who move through his poems. In Herrera's long poem "A Day Without a Mexican" (a response to the California-wide pro-immigrant demonstrations of 2006), "a Chicano friar dressed / in blue-black tunic stands / by the overpass," and Herrera asks

who will save us

who will save him

is there still room for America to be saved? he hands me a can for change with the figure of el Santo Niño de Atocha

little omchild holy in a colonial dress of angelic powders
the boy my mother Lucha led me to at Guadalupe church in
    Logan Heights, San Diego, 1958

play play another guitar brother. . . .

the flow of jelly wire hearts the blood
churns the light burns this reading skin

Then there are the poems that begin simply by naming the people they want to portray: the poem extends, or defines, the personal name, almost as a dictionary definition extends the word at its head. James Merrill wrote the one-page poem "Manos Karastefanís" in the voice of the friend and lover, native to a Greek island, whom Merrill saw (so his biographer Langdon Hammer reports) as "almost a bodyguard." Merrill's version of Manos speaks right to you:

> Why are you smiling?
> I fought fair, I fought well,
> Not hurting my opponent
> To win this black belt.
>
> Why are you silent?
> I've brought you a white cheese
> From my island, and the sea's
> Voice in a shell.

Merrill has sewn an intricate pattern: everything rhymes or almost rhymes ("opponent"-"silent"; "well"-"belt"-"shell") even as the short lines, with no regular meter, suggest an articulate nonnative speaker of English, nervous, wanting to impress, stopping frequently, speaking to a lover who is also his social superior, trying to make sure he gets everything right.

Other poems name and define the poet. "Charles Simic," by Charles Simic, for example, reads, in part:

Charles Simic is a sentence.
A sentence has a beginning and an end. . . .

Who is writing this awkward sentence?
A blackmailer, a girl in love,
And an applicant for a job.

Simic is showing, concisely, how (to quote the novelist Rachel Hartman) "we are none of us just one thing": that's also one reason most poets write more than one poem. Other poets use their own names in other ways: Jaime Gil de Biedma's great modern Spanish poem "Después de la muerte de Jaime Gil de Biedma" ("After the Death of Jaime Gil de Biedma") asks how he would envision his own last days, depicting a melancholy would-be sybarite who is trying hard not to leave regrets.

Reading a poem can be sharing a set of feelings, but it can also feel like getting to know someone new. No wonder so many poets have introduced themselves by naming themselves in their poems. Like the self-portrait, the self-naming poem has a plethora of recent examples, among them Laura Kasischke's "Laura" and Ocean Vuong's "Someday I'll Love Ocean Vuong":

Ocean,
  are you listening? The most beautiful part
  of your body is wherever
  your mother's shadow falls.

All these poems—those that play on the poet's name and those that do not—work to say what is special, what is unusual, what is recognizable about the inner life of an individual, giving not just a unique social label (like "Charles Simic") but something like a mysterious true name. And true names, as anybody who has read Ursula K. Le Guin's Earthsea books knows, have power. You can show your true name, or your true self, to someone else, framing it for their ease or their benefit, or you can simply try to see yourself as you are.

The difference between this way of reading and the way of reading we saw in chapter 1, between poems that work as definitions of characters and poems that work as lyrics—and many poems can work as either, or both—is the difference between treating a poem as if it were a song you could sing and treating it as if it were a portrait or a biography. But poems of character focus on someone's interior life, as against the external events of a biography. As the poet Chris Price remarks, "A biography . . . is like the Louise Bourgeois sculpture of the cage in which are imprisoned a mirror and a pair of marble feet, eternally running away." A poem encapsulates a particular character, a particular life, and an alternative to that cage.

A half-truth, or a cliché, about lyric poetry—articulated by the nineteenth-century philosopher John Stuart Mill—holds that true poems take place in solitude and are never heard, only overheard. That's wrong for the poets who are most themselves in front of an audience (Donne, for example, or Yeats), wrong for Hufflepuffs, for extroverts, for any of us who need to listen to our friends in order to figure out who we are. But it's just right for the introverts, like Ammons or William Wordsworth, who feel that they are most themselves when they're alone. So Wordsworth suggests, at least, in a famous poem usually called "Daffodils":

I wandered lonely as a cloud
That floats on high o'er vales and hills,
When all at once I saw a crowd,
A host, of golden daffodils;
Beside the lake, beneath the trees,
Fluttering and dancing in the breeze.

The rest of the poem considers the way that the daffodils live on in Wordsworth's memory: "They flash upon that inward eye / Which is the bliss of solitude" and contribute to his mysterious inner life.

This book describes six reasons to read some poems, six frames into which a lot of poems I like might fit; it does not describe six nonoverlapping categories—some poems can be read for feeling and characters, just as others can be read for feeling and form, or for characters and wisdom. As we make our way through these reasons, these examples, we need to keep in mind that one reason to read one poem, one category into which a poem fits, does not exclude all the others; that's especially important when a poet has been pigeonholed, or stereotyped, or read for just one reason for too many years. (We'll see a few poets like that later in this book.) Of course "Daffodils" is a lyric poem. Of course Wordsworth, wandering, shares a host of emotions: delight in solitude, exhilaration, and (later, in "The Solitary Reaper") the sense of losing oneself in one's own memories. "That music in my heart I bore," he concludes, "long after it was heard no more." And yet most of us would not view daffodils in this way, or not often. The poem also says a lot about who *he* is.

And you don't have to like him. The William Wordsworth of "Daffodils," though he praised solitude, probably did not glimpse those bright flowers alone: he was out walking with his sister Dorothy, whose meticulous journals (unpublished during her lifetime), with their generous descriptions of nature, gave her brother the basis for some of his poems. The present-day poet Jennifer Chang wrote a snarky poem called "Dorothy Wordsworth" about her:

> The daffodils can go fuck themselves.
> I'm tired of their crowds, yellow rantings
> about the spastic sun that shines and shines
> and shines. How are they any different
>
> from me? I, too, have a big messy head
> on a fragile stalk. I spin with the wind.

Chang speaks (albeit in modern English) for Dorothy; she can set them both—as underappreciated writers, as quiet complainers, and also as women—against William's easily mockable ego and against "the critics" (Chang's term), who like clichés about spring:

> They know the old joy,
> that wakeful quotidian, the dark plot
> of future growing things, each one
> labeled *Narcissus nobilis* or *Jennifer Chang*.

Narcissus nobilis is the daffodil's botanical name; narcissism may be the poet's problem.

Langston Hughes gets introduced—often to very young readers—as a representative poet of black America, and that's not wrong, but it's remarkably limiting: he, too, understood that no one is just one thing. And he created multiple characters, often through bits of imagined conversation. His great book-length poem *Montage of a Dream Deferred* often gets quoted for the same authoritative, impersonal line ("What happens to a dream deferred?"). In fact, though, *Montage* is a crowd of distinctive voices whose characters may communicate their quintessence in only a few lines: "Be-Bop Boys," for example, whose three-line poem rhymes "Mecca" (the holy city of Islam) with "Decca" (the record label). Hughes also created recurring characters, giving them more space to say who they are. The wry, worldly Madam Alberta K. Johnson, for example, has had to learn to take care of herself:

He said, Madam, I swear
All I want is you.
Right then and there
I knowed we were through!

I told him, Jackson,
You better leave—
You got some'n else
Up your sleeve.

Does Hughes agree with this dismissal of romantic love? Maybe, and maybe not; the point is not what the poet might think but what impression we get from Alberta K. Johnson, with her mild swagger, her assertive rhyme, her defiance and self-reliance. (She's heard, and dismissed, men with similar claims before.)

•

I have been describing people, characters, selves, and also (in chapter 1) feelings and states of mind, as if they were at least as real as apples and hedgehogs, or else as real as laws and civil rights. But you cannot photograph or weigh a soul or a self (or a civil right). Poets involved in up-to-the-minute philosophy or literary theory will sometimes tell you that there is no such thing as a soul, or a self, or a civil right; that "I" and "you" and perhaps "we" are names for illusions; that the best explanations for human actions and human emotions involve social forces or networks, along with the bodies that they and their powers move through. When you write a poem, after all, you are putting together words and phrases and forms and ideas that have already been used hundreds or thousands of times by somebody else. The same thing is true when you write a personal letter, or ask somebody to marry you, or advocate on behalf of someone's civil rights.

For some poets all this history just doesn't matter: of course we combine old things in new ways to make lives and poems; of course we choose only from the resources available. For other poets it matters a great deal: it makes the portrayal of a consistent, individual character (in first person or third) misleading, or impossible, or possible only with carve-outs and philosophical caveats. "Poetry can be heard to stagger under a weight of self-portrayal," writes the British thinker and poet Denise Riley, "having taken that as its sole and proper object." Riley, in her terrific and challenging book of prose and verse called *The Words of Selves*, cannot escape her sense that she is not exactly a single person, since her thoughts and feelings come to her, or to "her," already made out of the words and the concepts she finds in others' work: self-portraits can only, at best, recycle materials. Of her own poems, she says, "I append my signature sheepishly because I know I am a sounding chamber in poetry, even more than in prose." She feels like an echo chamber, a collage: "What if this discontinuous legacy in self-telling became the topic of a poem itself?" That poem might sound like Riley's own:

> Could I try on that song of my sociologised self? Its
> Long angry flounce, tuned to piping self-sorrow, flopped
> Lax in my gullet—"But we're all *bufo bufo*." I sobbed—
> Suddenly charmed by community—"all warty we are."

Bufo bufo is the common European toad. Writing poetry has turned her not into a fully realized individual but into an awkward amphibian, indistinguishable from the rest.

People who are used to feeling erased, or overlooked, or treated unjustly en masse, may object that we go to poems precisely to feel that we are real, that our selves matter: the last thing we want from a poem is to hear that no one is real, that selves don't exist. Indeed many poems—the poems we call lyric; quite a lot of performed modern poetry, too— try very hard to show how people (the poet, the reader, a created character) are unique, significant, real: to show that (as the poet, essayist, and rapper Kyle "Guante" Tran Myrhe put it) "when they look right through you, you're still there." And yet you don't have to be a philosopher or (like Riley) an academic thinker to feel that your unique self—if you even have one—doesn't stand still or can't fit into any one set of words. The twenty-first-century poet

Laura Mullen compares her own poems to self-portraits in sand, "the dream of being perfectly understood coagulating briefly into grainy legibility." You might see yourself, too, as partly illegible, hidden, incomprehensible, a lousy fit for any single symbol. You might feel like more than one thing, or more than one person, at once.

You can find poems whose figures of speech dramatize this disposition too. The Welsh collection of legends called *The Mabinogion* (no younger than the eleventh century) gives its archetypal poet Taliesin the power of self-transformation, so he can act out the variety within us. In D. W. Nash's translation:

> I have been a drop in the air.
> I have been a shining star.
> I have been a word in a book. . . .
> I have been the string of a harp,
> Enchanted for a year
> In the foam of water.
> I have been a poker in the fire.
> I have been a tree in a covert.
> There is nothing in which I have not been.

It might be exciting, or else disconcerting, to be so volatile, to feel capable of such interior multiplicity, such change. If you don't find that kind of vertigo in Taliesin's song, you can certainly find it in John Berryman's modern update, in which the poet sees himself first as one person and then as another, until we learn that he's best defined by the constant churn in who he thinks he is. Here is the start of Berryman's Dream Song 22:

I am the little man who smokes & smokes.
I am the girl who does know better but.
I am the king of the pool.
I am so wise I had my mouth sewn shut.
I am a government official & a goddamned fool.
I am a lady who takes jokes.

Yet this catalog form, this way of creating a character through disconcertingly open-ended lists, does not have to feel disorienting. C. D. Wright made it charming; her poem called "Personals" combines the "I am" list-poem à la Berryman and Taliesin with the outward form of a personal ad, the kind that filled the back pages of daily and weekly newspapers before the advent of Craigslist:

Some nights I sleep with my dress on. My teeth
are small and even. I don't get headaches.
Since 1971 or before, I have hunted a bench
where I could eat my pimento cheese in peace.
If this were Tennessee and across that river, Arkansas,
I'd meet you in West Memphis tonight. We could
have a big time. Danger, shoulder soft.

Few poets have done more in fewer syllables to show us who they are, what they are like, what it's like to be them. Of course we can't ever know that—we are not telepaths— but we can't be sure we know our real-life, in-person friends either. We can, though, get the sense that we have come close—in real life, through repeated and trusting interaction;

in poetry like Wright's, though linguistic nuance (she wants to have not a good or great time but a "big time").

Some of that nuance shows how thoroughly our tools for describing ourselves depend not just on sound and language but on culturally specific references. Wright (who grew up in the Ozarks and settled in Rhode Island) converts local knowledge into personal puns. The soft shoulder belongs to the badly maintained road but also to Wright herself. Proper nouns later on in the poem include "Admiral Benbow," the name of a southern motel chain. Such details—not just the motel chain but the pimento cheese—are the kind you'd use for a password, the kind that only intimates would know. That's why the poem—like other Wright poems—generates, at least for many readers, an effect of lightning intimacy, a feeling that this is someone you'd want to meet.

As fast-paced, digressive, inventive as it is, Wright's poem also imagines—like Williams's "The Last Words of My English Grandmother," like Wordsworth's "Daffodils," like Hughes's Alberta K. Johnson poem—a human person's speech (the Wordsworth of "Daffodils" seems to speak to himself). Poets can also see themselves in animals and objects that are not persons, that would never speak except in a poem or a myth or a fantasy novel. Riley saw her baffled and protean self as a toad among other toads. "Self-Portrait as This or That" poems stand out, from this vantage point, only because they put their central symbol in the title. The oldest European talking-object poems are riddles, most of which challenge us to guess what speaks. Most of the surviving riddles in Anglo-Saxon (aka Old English) come from a manuscript called the Exeter Book. Riddle 33, in Paul F. Baum's modern English, begins:

> My head is   forged with the hammer,
> hurt with sharp tools,   smoothed by files.
> I take in my mouth   what is set before me.

The answer: a key.

Anglo-Saxon-style riddles persist to this day: Carter Revard, a scholarly authority on medieval European literature, also writes about his Osage and Ponca background. His original poems include riddles on Native objects, among them "What the Eagle Fan Says," which ends:

> now I move lightly   in a man's left hand,
> above dancing feet   follow the sun
> around old songs   soaring toward heaven
> on human breath,   and I help them rise.

Not all poems about objects, plants, or nonhuman animals make those things speak to us. Many contemporary poets work hard to make animals, in particular, seem irretrievably alien, not like ourselves. And yet the harder a poet works to give a personality to a nonhuman speaker—a talking seagull, a feathered fan from a Native ceremony, a doorknob—the more you might think that you are reading a portrait of a particular kind of human being. A pure and beautiful example is Elizabeth Bishop's "Giant Toad," part of her three-part prose poem "Rainy Season: Sub-Tropics." The toad's speech begins:

I am too big. Too big by far. Pity me.

My eyes bulge and hurt. They are my one great beauty, even so. They see too much, above, below. And yet, there is not much to see. The rain has stopped. The mist is gathering on my skin in drops. The drops run down my back, run from the corners of my downturned mouth, run down my sides and drip beneath my belly. Perhaps the droplets on my mottled hide are pretty, like dewdrops, silver on a moldering leaf? They chill me through and through.

One modern name for this toad's bad fit between self and world, for the feeling that it is always raining outside and you're always unsightly, is *dysphoria*. Another is *depression*. Another is *derealization*, the sense that you aren't real and do not inhabit your body, a sense that Riley's postmodern toads might exude too. But these terms do not show nearly enough about how these feelings work to form a character, how they interact with the other characteristics that might make you who you are or make you feel like a giant toad. For that we have sentences, metaphors, details, poems.

Sometimes one persona, or one personification, drives an entire poem, portraying the whole of a character through one extended metaphor. The thing or creature personified may be real and minutely observed (as in Bishop), or fantastic, or science fictional. Here are the second stanza and the final lines of Jane Yeh's "On Being an Android":

How I was made: equal parts mystery and on-off switches.
Age 5: driving lessons, triathlon, med school, embroidery.

Everyone says looks don't matter, as long as you've got
    personality.
My first crush was a Roomba I mistook for a person.
Second crush: a person, but don't even go there. . . .

Being human means the whole world is made for you like
    a cake.
Being an android means you get some cake, but you can't
    eat it.
I don't know how to flirt, so the bears at my local are
    teaching me.

The lightning in my head means a brainstorm is coming.
If I think hard enough about anything, my hair starts to curl.
It's easy to predict the future when there's a timer in your
    neck.
The instruction manual says my knee can be used as a utensil.
Everyone admires my artificial skin, but nobody wants to
    touch it.

Yeh's lines are funny until, suddenly, if they fit you, they
are not. Her independent sentences unspool down the page
almost like lines in a computer program, like parts of a test
or a self-diagnostic list ("local" in British English is a neighborhood pub). The awkwardness, the first crushes, suggest an
android still in their teens who finds it hard to be a teen. And
these lines can speak to certain teens—and certain adults—
with special force. Some people on the autism spectrum, and
some who identify as trans, like me, and some people who are
both (a disproportionate number of us are both) have long
felt like androids or like nonhuman bodies without being

able to articulate why. We may see ourselves here, at last, in a poem about being this person, this sort of atypical person, and plug ourselves in.

Talking objects—hammers, toads, or androids—may stand for one person or for one kind of person; they may stand alone, one object per poem. But they can also speak to one another, as in William Blake's "The Clod and the Pebble":

"Love seeketh not Itself to please,
Nor for itself hath any care;
But for another gives its ease
And builds a Heaven in Hell's despair."

So sang a little Clod of Clay
Trodden with the cattle's feet,
But a Pebble of the brook
Warbled out these metres meet.

"Love seeketh only Self to please,
To bind another to Its delight:
Joys in another's loss of ease,
And builds a Hell in Heaven's despite."

Is true love as selfless as the first stanza asserts? Do you want your beloved to care only for you, to give up everything else, all other desires? Would you do the same thing for him, her, or them? Have you tried? The clod—the character, the archetype there—thinks it's not love if you won't (so to speak) let your lover walk all over you. But that's not how Blake thinks: it's how "a little Clod of Clay" thinks, and of course clay would think that way. Cattle will trample clay anyway, whether it claims to enjoy being stepped on or tries to protest (compare the stepped-on housewives of Betty Friedan's *The Feminine Mystique*). A pebble—which won't change its form (at least not visibly) no matter how long the stream flows over it—would naturally have another opinion: that hard or hardened and utterly selfish lover will remain unchanged and unmoved. And neither kind of love would "please," or even "ease," the lovers whom Blake's poem, taken as a whole, might let you envision, lovers who ought to take each other's pleasures and each other's whole lives into account. It's as if Blake were commenting on the limits of the talking-object poem while writing that poem: human persons ought to be more flexible, and stranger, than any single vocalized stand-in will let us be.

Other poets portray themselves by telling stories—or parts of stories—about the most distinctive or most painful parts of their lives. That kind of poetry sometimes gets called "confessional." Roman Catholic churchgoers confess their sins to a priest from behind a mesh, grate, or partition that allows the parishioner to be heard but not seen. Confessional poetry in the stricter sense (as introduced by the critic M. L. Rosenthal) imagines not the telling of sins to a priest but the telling of shameful life secrets to a psychoanalyst, as if those secrets explained who you truly are.

Writers like Riley react against confessional poetry on political as well as philosophical grounds: if we want to know what's gone wrong with our own lives, we need to look at society, not just at our own biographies. And yet those biographies—sifted, arranged, and reframed in poems—can point to solutions: so many lives seem wounded in similar ways. You may be yourself at your finest, your most sincere, but you are also constructed, mediated, synthesized, almost as pop songs can offer real, intense emotion by recombining artificial—synthesized—sounds. Indeed, you can show who you are in part through combining those sounds: Natalie Shapero's "Winter Injury," a self-portrait made of disconnected details (with an eye to Wright's "Personals"), concludes with a jarring half-rhyme that is itself a great example of Shapero's wary unease, her sense that she has been manipulated, that she is not quite herself: "My old love handled me hard. I let it happen. / The songs I like are mostly swears and clapping." She has not heard, and does not want to hear, her own voice.

Can a confessional poet—one whose "I" appears to be the author, one who tells painfully personal life stories—also show us the constraints of a wider society, the way that its permissions and prohibitions have made us who we are? Of course she can: Brenda Shaughnessy's book *So Much Synth*, about motherhood, girlhood, Asian American identity, and pop music fandom in 1980s California, brings the confessional mode forward from the 1950s and 1960s into our day. Shaughnessy's cascade of unrhymed couplets—sometimes fluent, sometimes painful to hear—returns to the roughest spots of the poet's teens, touching on topics from period blood to sexual harassment. Her poems invoke 1980s pop songs along with teenage diaries: in high school,

You couldn't just be yourself anywhere.

There was an amazing story in me, one that I would live powerfully in wet velvet poetry: *And you wanted*

to dance so I asked you to dance, but fear is in our soul. . . .
the voice of Simon Le Bon permeated all those

new cells, the bloody ones, the ripenings, and I knew
his love was deep.

Le Bon was the lead singer of Duran Duran, whose 1983 hit "Is There Something I Should Know?" shares its title with Shaughnessy's long, fierce 2016 poem. It is as if the verse form and the reference to apparently frivolous and artificial (but in fact deeply moving) pop music make possible the kind of truth-telling, and the kind of harsh rebellion, that the poet wishes she had seen and shared back then. Like the Hayes of *American Sonnets* and like Riley, Shaughnessy addresses directly the way that her unique, identifiable self, the character who speaks right to us from the poems, is at once unique and typical, artificial and real, not just embarrassing but staged, or stagy:

Who was I kidding? Even in my private diary
I performed myself to an audience of one, no one.

A stock character playing to an empty house,
though I'd no theater experience at all.

I lied outright, wrote daydreams as if true,
was all-knowing and exquisite, simultaneously

the worst person ever to have lived. Adolescence
is all absolutes: if bad, one must be the very worst

to avoid being mistaken for average.
To be ordinary was just being invisible,

and surely slow naked death by ants hurts less than that.

It's a cliché about teenage diaries that we think we are the worst, or the best, or the most hurt, or the loneliest, when really so many people feel just like us—and it is not just teens for whom that's true. To this portrait of her vulnerable teen self, Shaughnessy adds the teenage (and not only teenage) twist of wanting to stand out; that's part of her character too.

But is it OK to want to stand out? Is the ambition to represent yourself, or your feelings, or your individuality, in poetry no more than a wish for glory or fame? (John Milton, three hundred years before Brenda Shaughnessy, chastised his own sharp hopes for fame, "that last infirmity of noble mind.") Does wanting to be a famous artist—a pop star or an actor or a poet—mean participating in a system so bad as to be irredeemable? If lyric poems and poems of character represent people, is it wrong to want yours to come across as exceptional, or exceptionally beautiful? You might call your friend beautiful, but you would not (I hope) argue at length about exactly how beautiful, and only a wicked witch would spend time wondering who is the fairest of them all.

Is it, then, wrong to ask what makes a poem stand out, or which poem is the best, or the strongest, or the most beautiful? If the answer to that question seems too easy, consider the contemporary poet Vandana Khanna, who sees her poems, and everyone else's poems, as very much like individual people:

My poetry walks around with brown skin and turmeric under its nails. It refuses to sit down and be quiet because it's a girl. . . . My poetry stopped trying to be "normal" even though it wanted to when it was growing up. Now, it might make you uncomfortable: you might have to look away or shift a little in your seat, you might pretend not to hear it or "get" it, which is OK because my poetry doesn't blend in. It will stand out like a sore in the room. It will be foreign and not apologize. You won't know what box to put it in and it won't make it on to your list of "approved" readings because it shows you a world where no face looks like yours.

There is no way out of this trap about value and beauty if you insist on judging poems about characters (and about feelings) by a single standard, ranking them like chickens at a state fair or figure skaters at the Olympics. But poetry isn't the state fair, nor is it figure skating (though we will see some parallels to judged sports like skating in chapter 3). There is no single standard, and no single contest decides what should or will last. You can like multiple poems for multiple, sometimes incompatible reasons, just as you can like multiple human beings, and you can—I try to—seek out and listen carefully both to poems whose inward characters, whose imaginary human beings, show you a face that looks like yours (for me that includes Yeh's android and Bishop's toad), and to poems whose faces look like nothing and no one you have seen before. Some will sound unruly, or awkward, or incompatible with older standards of beauty; some will sound glossy and synthesized; and some will have turmeric under their nails.

•

All these kinds of poems—the "I am" list à la Taliesin, the self-portrait, the talking object, the confessional poem of traumatic memory—introduce a character close up, from the inside: you can imagine that character thinking or speaking, envision yourself with their portrait or face-to-face. Other poems portray a character from the outside, showing you how a trustworthy observer, or a close friend, or a crew of people, knew them. Often that person is dead: the poem works as eulogy, as a commemoration, like Samuel Johnson's characteristically sober 1782 poem "On the Death of Dr. Robert Levet." Read it slowly, please:

Condemned to Hope's delusive mine,
    As on we toil from day to day,
By sudden blasts, or slow decline,
    Our social comforts drop away.

Well tried through many a varying year,
    See Levet to the grave descend;
Officious, innocent, sincere,
    Of every friendless name the friend.

Yet still he fills Affection's eye,
    Obscurely wise, and coarsely kind;
Nor, lettered Arrogance, deny
    Thy praise to merit unrefined.

When fainting Nature called for aid,
    And hovering Death prepared the blow,
His vigorous remedy displayed
    The power of art without the show.

In Misery's darkest cavern known,
    His useful care was ever nigh,
Where hopeless Anguish poured his groan,
    And lonely Want retired to die.

No summons mocked by chill delay,
  No petty gain disdained by pride,
The modest wants of every day
  The toil of every day supplied.

His virtues walked their narrow round,
  Nor made a pause, nor left a void;
And sure the Eternal Master found
  The single talent well employed.

The busy day, the peaceful night,
  Unfelt, uncounted, glided by;
His frame was firm, his powers were bright,
  Though now his eightieth year was nigh.

Then with no throbbing fiery pain,
  No cold gradations of decay,
Death broke at once the vital chain,
  And freed his soul the nearest way.

To understand what made Levet special for Johnson, it helps to understand (and it's in this poem) how Johnson saw life. We are miners for hope who dig up nothing worth keeping; life is a kind of bondage, a trial ("well tried"), and those best suited to it are not those who love it most but those determined to ignore its niceties and do what we were put on earth to do. So Johnson asserts, with end-stopped lines like piled bricks, supported by the strict meter of Protestant hymns. Dr. Levet, we learn, was just such a person: rude, without the graces of formal education, of limited abilities even within his chosen profession, he did all he could for the people who came to need him, the London poor to whom he provided medical services free of charge. "The single talent well employed" is Levet's own talent for treating the injured and sick, as well as the talent, or coin, in the Gospels (for example, Matthew 25:14–30), which Jesus warns us not to bury but to invest. Someone "officious," as Levet was, might bustle and demand respect, but he might also attend to his duties, his "offices." At a cocktail party, you might yearn to have somebody free you from Levet's company; if you had bronchitis in Cheapside in 1764, there might be nobody you'd rather see. Johnson as poet and critic loved to generalize, to make sweeping statements in Latinate terms. That habit of generalization also fits Levet: it generates concision, brushing away imagined details in the same way that Levet himself did what mattered, kept busy, until Death or God or mercy "freed his soul."

In showing you (so far) two reasons for reading poems—to share feelings and to discover characters—I have also been showing you some of the kinds and categories into which readers have long sorted them. These categories need not be any stranger than the ones that we use for pop music, where there are power ballads, club bangers, trip-hop, pop-punk, electro, and so on, as well as breakup songs, kiss-off songs, slow jams, et cetera; some musical kinds are identified by attitude or by the singer's apparent purpose, others by tempo, rhythm, instrumentation. And as in pop music (where you can have an electro anthem but also an electro ballad) one poem can belong to several categories. You can see further into many poems if you ask yourself what kind, or kinds, of poem you've got in front of you. A cry of despair? An invitation? A funeral elegy? A poem on the occasion of someone's birth? A kind of pure meditative lyric, speech to the self with no occasion at all?

Is it a self-portrait, or a compact portrait of someone else, or a figurative portrait (poet as raindrop, poet as toad)? Is it a speech, delivered as if to a listener, as if the character were in a play?

That last kind of poem has a well-traced history. Invented in the mid-nineteenth century, these kinds of poems, called dramatic monologues, imagine a character speaking in real time to a physically present audience, with asides that help the reader imagine what or who else is onstage. The most famous dramatic monologue is Robert Browning's "My Last Duchess" (1842), whose speaker turns out to be a cartoon villain, a megalomaniacal Italian count who had his first wife murdered out of petty jealousy. Alert readers gradually realize how evil Browning's count must be, making deductions from nothing except his own words. Browning's more introspective, more character-driven, and (to my mind) emotionally richer dramatic monologues appeared later, in *Men and Women* (1855). Two of his best go together; they are two sides of a large and detailed coin, two individuated figures whose lives and personalities give two takes on realism, individuality, sex, and the nature and purpose of art.

The paired monologues speak for, or impersonate, two real painters from Renaissance Florence, "Fra Lippo Lippi" and "Andrea del Sarto"; the painters have the same names as the poems, though art galleries usually call the former painter Filippo or Filippino Lippi, without the "Fra" (which means "Brother"; he is a monk). Browning's Fra Lippo becomes a cheerful, even rumbustious exponent of painterly realism. He loves to see and think about and depict (and, sometimes, touch) food and drink and human faces and bodies, and he has become very good at observing them. As a child, he had to be:

But, mind you, when a boy starves in the streets
Eight years together, as my fortune was,
Watching folk's faces to know who will fling
The bit of half-stripped grape-bunch he desires,
And who will curse or kick him for his pains . . .
Why, soul and sense of him grow sharp alike,
He learns the look of things, and none the less
For admonition from the hunger-pinch.

He learned to read faces and characters as a child beggar because if he could not do so, he would not eat. For the same
reason he learned to value material things: food for hunger,
drink for thirst. Fra Lippo entered a monastery for food and
shelter: monks took him in as a child and fed him with the
assumption that he would grow up in their order. But the
monks do not admire his painting; it is too vivid, too individuated, too sensuous. They tell Fra Lippo (in his unfriendly
paraphrase):

Your business is not to catch men with show,
With homage to the perishable clay,
But lift them over it, ignore it all,
Make them forget there's such a thing as flesh.

Fra Lippo defends the level of detail and the exuberance
that Lippo's paintings share with Browning's own poem. The
poem tries to show how it feels to love what he loves, to
hunger as he has hungered, and maybe to lust as he lusts (he
may have been paying for sex), as well as to see intensely, as
he sees:

Why can't a painter lift each foot in turn,
Left foot and right foot, go a double step,
Make his flesh liker and his soul more like,
Both in their order? Take the prettiest face,
The Prior's niece . . . patron-saint—is it so pretty
You can't discover if it means hope, fear,
Sorrow or joy? won't beauty go with these?
Suppose I've made her eyes all right and blue,
Can't I take breath and try to add life's flash,
And then add soul and heighten them three-fold?

The breaths and onrushing phrases in the poem might
help you envision the face, the body, from which the words
come. "This world's no blot for us," Lippo continues, "Nor
blank; it means intensely, and means good: / To find its meaning is my meat and drink." To paint or describe anything or
anyone enthusiastically, with attention to its uniqueness, for
Lippo (as, it seems, for Browning), is to help us love the world
God made.

"Andrea del Sarto," the character and the poem named
after him, are the tragedy to Lippo's comedy, the eternal dissatisfaction to set against Lippo's cycle of hunger, joy, and sati-
ety. Andrea may be wrong about himself—indeed, he has lied
to himself for much of his life. And yet, just as much as Fra
Lippo, he lets us think honestly about how poems delineate
character and about what a poem of character—in this case,
another dramatic monologue—might do. It can introduce us
to the interior life, the disposition, the temperament, the ob-
sessive thoughts and hidden motives, of singularly imagined

people who may or may not seem familiar, who may or may not much resemble us.

Andrea's nickname (and Browning's subtitle) is "the faultless painter," meaning not that he was blameless (he was not blameless) but that his paintings had no technical flaws. Fra Lippo was a gifted technician too: he painted in blooming color, loved life, loved his life. Andrea does not love his life. He tells himself that he loves his wife, Lucrezia, who does not love him back and never has; she likes the money his artistic talent can earn. He has come to understand that artistic talent, without vision or heart, can never be enough. "'Tis easy, all of it! / No sketches first, no studies, that's long past: / I do what many dream of all their lives." And yet, he tells Lucrezia (while she gets dressed to go out and gamble without him, marring his wet paint with her flowing gown), he feels inferior to painters who possess far less craft, and less knowledge, than he:

> There burns a truer light of God in them,
> In their vexed beating stuffed and stopped-up brain,
> Heart, or whate'er else, than goes on to prompt
> This low-pulsed forthright craftsman's hand of mine.
> Their works drop groundward, but themselves, I know,
> Reach many a time a heaven that's shut to me

And so the pouty monologue moves forward, mixing profound introspection about the nature and purpose of art with self-pity and unacknowledged irony, right up to an exclamation still frequently quoted and frequently misunderstood: "Ah, but a man's reach should exceed his grasp, / Or what's a heaven for?" Andrea is not so much encouraging us, or himself, as admitting that he can never reach his heaven, a heaven of passion realized and returned. He has settled for bad, self-deluding rewards by painting for money, and for Lucrezia, on earth.

Something of Andrea's self-defeating nature, as well as of his very careful brushwork, comes across in the muted or hushed sounds of his poem, both when he speaks of his art and when he speaks of Lucrezia's "low voice my soul hears, as a bird / The fowler's pipe, and follows to the snare." She really has ensnared him. But the details of her machinations lie outside the house he cannot leave, outside the emotional space in which Browning concentrates on Andrea's own character.

Andrea has often been read as a monstrous figure drowning in self-pity; Fra Lippo, as Browning's all-out defense of his art. Readers who care for Browning's pair of painters, though, can see in them not just individual figures, delineated with rare verve—one comedic and boisterous, the other defeated, hemmed in—but also a pair of poems about the use of artistic technique, about why we care for other people (in poems, in fiction, in real life), and about the value of art.

Andrea's musings, after all, match or anticipate the musings of later poets who wonder what good they have done, what might be the point of their labors, whether they have wasted their lives. The modern poet Wallace Stevens asked— in one of the last poems he finished—"I wonder, have I lived a skeleton's life / As a disbeliever in reality, // A countryman of all the bones in the world?" Such wondering, and such sadness—inseparable from his gift for abstraction—helped to make Stevens the poet he was, just as Herrera's garrulousness and Bishop's hesitancy made them who they were, and their language reflects it. Hughes's Madame Johnson tells us who she is with every syllable. Andrea's mellifluous language, like his style of painting ("all is silver-grey . . . the worse!"), reflects who he is, too.

We have seen ways in which several kinds of poem can introduce us to people, some real, some imagined, some identified tacitly or unmistakably with the poets themselves. But you don't have to read all poems for their characters; you can read other poems—or some of the same poems— in quest of other pleasures. I have said that poets are not figure skaters: if you rank them all on a points scale, you're doing it wrong. But in another way poets are very much like figure skaters, and like point guards, and like painters (like Fra Lippo and like Andrea): they do something quite difficult with a medium that took them time to master, something that you can seek out and appreciate—if you so choose—for its techniques, its forms and patterns. You can ignore these techniques or take them for granted at first, but you are going to learn to recognize them if you spend a lot of time around poems; you might also find more poems to enjoy, and more ways to enjoy them, by looking at form and technique first.

chapter three

FORMS

D O YOU WATCH BASKETBALL, OR FIGURE SKATING, OR both? Do you cook not just for sustenance but am-bitiously, making dishes with thirty ingredients? Do any of your favorite musicians or bands stand out not just for originality or expression but also for their technical chops, for the speed or versatility with which they play their instru-ments? Do you knit, or have friends who knit and who show you their work?

If the answer to any of these questions is yes, you already know how to enjoy technique: how to like, or love, works for the skill that they display in following challenging forms. Any poem worth your time has, in some sense, a form; patterns of long and short sentences, repeated or discarded words, even short and long breaths, mark even the most chaotic, one-of-a-kind, or apparently improvised work. Much of the time, though, when you return to a given poem for its technical mastery, its formal accomplishment, for moments that make you say not so much "That's profound!" or "That's me!" but "Wow!" or "Oh, I didn't know you could do that with language!" you will be looking for patterns that are easier to talk about or to recognize; you might, for example, be looking at a lattice of repeated words, or at supercomplex syntax, or at networks of rhymes.

Poems that offer nothing but technique may seem too easy to write or too hard: they are exquisite shells with no animals inside, a "sad mechanic exercise" (to quote Tennyson). But we can admire a particular animal for its pearlescent shell; we can admire poets, no less than athletes or musicians, for their technique as well as for their heart, which is to say, for the way that they accomplish something determined by constraints, by rules about what you can do, and how, and when.

This chapter looks at those kinds of constraints, some old, some new, and at the patterns that they make possible. Some of them—say, an alliterative line (one that repeats consonants at the fronts of words)—show up in distinct moments within poems, like one pass or one shot in a basketball game. Others, like a sonnet form, dictate the shape of a whole poem, analogous to a whole skating routine. "We fill preexisting forms," writes Frank Bidart, "and by filling them we change them and are changed." To read poetry for technique, for formal accomplishment—inside and outside of famous old forms, some of which have familiar names—is to see how forms interact with ideas, characters, and emotions, and to see how, given time, the forms themselves change.

This chapter starts out with some thoughts on technique in general. I look next at short poems that rely on rhymes and the patterns and symmetries rhymes create, and at poems that not only demonstrate formal beauty but defend it through the arguments they contain. I show how some poems revel in their artificiality, their lack of resemblance to natural things, and how others tie their formal beauty to nature.

Forms come to us with individual histories. I look at rhyming forms that come to us from the European past, then at others from several parts of Asia. I look at poets who adhere to conventions and at poets who surpass them; at poets who see forms as ways to show off and at others who treat them almost as magic rituals, as forms of psychic escape. No form's past, these poems show, can predict its future; part of the fun in seeing how poets use forms, and part of their moral force, lies in how poets react to—and sometimes reject—a form's history. I conclude with kinds of technical power, kinds of formal satisfaction, that come from new forms, forms that modern poets made up: one involves leaving out vowels, while another makes mathematical and musical patterns from numbers of syllables, showing intricacies available no other way.

•

A poet who uses form well is playing a game, and play means adapting to preexisting constraints: that poet can "take an object, event, situation, or scenario [the sonnet, say] that wasn't designed for [them] and then *treat it as if it were*," to quote the video-game designer and philosopher Ian Bogost (italics his). The more restrictive the situation, the tougher the rules, the more impressive the play becomes. When you read poems for the personae within them, you are treating them almost as if the poems were people; when you read them for form, you treat them as games that poets can play. And play—formal excellence combined with creativity—requires rules, ways of "working a system ... in a new way" (Bogost again). We may delight in seeing poets do, within rules, something we thought nobody could do, something only that poet, in that poem, could do—whether the rules are as familiar as basketball rules to a baller or sonata rules to a classical pianist, or whether the rules are ones the poet made up just now.

Bogost adds that (at least up to a point) "the more constraints we add ... the more interesting the result." A three-line poem where all the lines end on the same word or the same rhyme might be fun; a thirty-line poem where all the lines use the same rhyme or end on the same word or its homonyms would be a lot more fun, or more impressive, as long as it also sounds like a poem with some emotion behind it too, not—or not only—like a stunt. If it doesn't sound like something is at stake—like there's some reason to read *besides* achieved form—then you are not likely to re-read. Conversely, if it does sound like something's at stake—like the form fits a person we care about; like there's some emotion that fits these words or some passionate project that's right for them—then the poet has done something impressive; she's made the form seem as if it were designed for her, and the tougher the form, the more impressive the poem. Only some poems work that way. But they have their own delights.

Looking at poems for technique first means looking at—noticing the properties specific to—a particular language. "Poetry is that which gets lost in translation," Robert Frost claimed, and many others have joined him; some medieval

Arabic scholars claimed that true poetry could be written only in Arabic, so beautiful were the rhythms and forms that that language alone permitted. Really, though, all languages let writers and speakers make patterns; some patterns are possible in many languages, some in just one or a few. The most obvious patterns in many older English poems, and in some new poems, are often rhymes or effects (like shared vowels or shared consonants) that feel like rhymes, even if not at the ends of lines.

Rhyme and its cousins thus make a good place to start thinking about technique, about how poets play within constraints. Frost's famous quip that free (meterless, rhymeless) verse is like tennis with no net falls apart once you see that free verse has its own rules; T. S. Eliot's almost equally snarky remark that "vers libre [that is, free verse] does not exist" holds up far better, since he meant just that verse without rhyme or meter must establish patterns of other sorts. In English, rhyme and meter are only the oldest and the easiest-to-see examples of line-by-line form and technique. The first half of this chapter will look almost entirely at how poets use rhyme, *not* (and I want to underline this point with a big red Sharpie) because rhyme is necessary for virtuoso form, but because learning to recognize how rhyme works, what patterns rhyme and rhyme-like euphonies enable, can help us think about technique in general. The second half will move on to more recently invented forms.

Here are some short passages by one of my favorite contemporary Irish poets, David Wheatley, writing about a graveyard in the gray, cloudy city of Aberdeen, Scotland, where he lives: "Grey that framed us living frames us gone / who lay cut flowers on granite, as though the stone / itself were what we'd honored all along." The trio of end rhymes or vowel rhymes ("gone," "stone," "along") locks itself into a larger matrix of repeated sounds, repeated words, and initial consonances ("gr," "wh"). And the only word without a good match is, fittingly, "cut": the living feel cut off from the newly dead.

Wheatley has something to show us, something to say: he seeks a dignity of address, a grim hearkening, that fits Aberdeen's stony cityscape. And yet to enjoy Wheatley's poem is (at least for me) to enjoy, first and last, all those patterns of sound. Here is another example of Wheatley's, called "Memory":

> the cloud of your passing
>   passed close and low
> a bird's shadow
>   where no bird flew

Clouds pass overhead; people pass away; their survivors are brought low. Wheatley's "low" and "flew" are half-rhymes; his net of puns and euphonies lifts suddenly so we can ask what we heard, what we missed.

The sound patterns in these lines, their dense displays of technique, are what we hear first, the way we hear hooks in pop songs. Other sound patterns in other poems may take a few readings to pop out, especially if the poems that harbor those patterns have plots. We can appreciate those patterns anyway once we step back to see how they work. Consider Langston Hughes's 1926 poem "Cross":

My old man's a white old man
And my old mother's black.
If ever I cursed my white old man
I take my curses back.

If ever I cursed my black old mother
And wished she were in hell,
I'm sorry for that evil wish
And now I wish her well.

My old man died in a fine big house.
My ma died in a shack.
I wonder where I'm going to die,
Being neither white nor black?

The last line points us back to the start of the poem (a device sometimes called ring composition): the title gives the answer to the question. This speaker, a racial "cross," will die on the cross, just like Jesus, another product of an unequal union, who died for our sins (and, also, led souls out of hell). Hughes threads his three quatrains with Trinitarian gestures: after the introductory couplet, with its three uses of "man," Hughes' biracial speaker gives us three curses in three lines, three wishes in three more, and three instances of "die" or "died," before concluding with the conundrum: "neither white nor black." Is it harder for him to be both white and black than it was for Jesus to be God and man? It might be. Hughes's figure is only human. You can love the poem first for its pointed critique of one society's racist hierarchies or for its elegant patterns, brought down on that society like a double-edged sword.

Hughes has reinvented the folk quatrain; Wheatley, the freestanding couplet. Both are forms that English-language poets have used at least since Chaucer (who brought it to England from the European continent). These poets play within rules they did not invent. Other poets cook up complex forms for their own one-time use. We met Robert Browning in chapter 2 as the king of the dramatic monologue. He also practiced the Victorian art of metrical experiment in short forms, fashioning effusive poems whose point was their play of sound: the most famous such poem begins, "Oh, to be in England, now that April's here!" Another, far less quoted and more exciting (to my ears), poem of that kind is "My Star":

> All that I know
>   Of a certain star,
> Is, it can throw
>   (Like the angled spar)
> Now a dart of red,
>   Now a dart of blue,
> Till my friends have said
>   They would fain see, too,
> My star that dartles the red and the blue!
> Then it stops like a bird,—like a flower, hangs furled;
>   They must solace themselves with the Saturn above it.
> What matter to me if their star is a world?
>   Mine has opened its soul to me; therefore I love it.

It's a love poem, of course; convention has it that Robert wrote it for Elizabeth Barrett Browning. Their elopement to Italy, their love letters, and her poems of their courtship,

Sonnets from the Portuguese, make one of the great Victorian love stories, and one with a happy ending. But the delights in "My Star" and the reasons for rereading it lie not in the whole of the love story but in the exuberance of the metrical and rhythmic variation. Rereading the poem is like hearing a pianist play 3/4 time with one hand, 7/8 with the other; like watching a basketball player's behind-the-back passes lead to repeated corner threes.

Browning moves fast until his eye and our ear lands on the long lines that describe the one star, the one that "darts" or "dartles." ("Spar" means "mica," or a similar mineral that can polarize light.) The same ear settles, as the lines fan out, as Browning moves from one difficult meter to another before settling in rough four-unit lines (da–da–DA, da–da–DA, da–da–DA, da–da–DA; the technical name is anapestic tetrameter). And then, just when you think Browning has constructed his quick, bright love poem along a two-part contrast between heaven and earth, or between star and star, or between his love and other people's bigger but less glorious, less personal affection—just then, Browning changes his rhythm again to introduce a third part. That final line has not four feet but five; it's not da–da–DA but da–DA (not anapests but iambs). That's how Browning's supposed "star" settles down with him.

Such beauty is its own excuse for being. That last sentence is not mine; it's Ralph Waldo Emerson's. If you know Emerson's writing already you may wonder why he belongs here, since Emerson did not want us to care about technique for its own sake: in his own words, "not metres but a metre-making argument" made for true poetry. His own poems sometimes get dinged for their lack of polish. And yet Emerson himself penned one of the great American defenses of beauty and pattern, "The Rhodora":

In May, when sea-winds pierced our solitudes,
I found the fresh Rhodora in the woods,
Spreading its leafless blooms in a damp nook,
To please the desert and the sluggish brook.
The purple petals, fallen in the pool,
Made the black water with their beauty gay;
Here might the red-bird come his plumes to cool,
And court the flower that cheapens his array.
Rhodora! if the sages ask thee why
This charm is wasted on the earth and sky,
Tell them, dear, that if eyes were made for seeing,
Then Beauty is its own excuse for being:
Why thou wert there, O rival of the rose!
I never thought to ask, I never knew:
But, in my simple ignorance, suppose
The self-same Power that brought me there brought you.

Emerson starts with couplets, then moves to quatrains, as if slowing down once he finds something worth a close look; he's also indulging in the very old poetic practice of pretending a flower can talk. The most famous poems that make flowers talk use roses, and perhaps misuse them. Edmund Waller's "Go, lovely Rose," for example, and Robert Herrick's "To the Virgins, to Make Much of Time" use flora to ask young women to yield to young men, since beauty in women, like beauty in flowers, won't last; it will wilt however you try to preserve it, so you should share it or give it away. Emerson will not use his red flower that way; he does not want to use it for anything, nor give it any meaning beyond itself, nor attribute to himself any stronger motive than simply letting it be, imagining an otherwise unknowable "Power" responsible for rhodora, rose, red-bird, sea, and writer, a power that also informs the beauty of the sounds in his unfolding lines.

Beauty is its own excuse for being, but it may not always defend itself; some poets set out explicitly to defend it, and to defend the near synonyms for beauty (prettiness, glamour, extravagance, attractiveness) that come with connotations of femininity, or weakness, or uselessness, or girliness. Angie Estes has made a career out of such defenses, presenting finely wrought, acoustically intricate cases for acoustic intricacy, craftwork, and flaunted skill, from Baroque sculpture to haute couture to poetry to parfumerie. These skills are, not to put too fine a point on it, sometimes sexy too. "True Confessions," the first poem in Estes's breakthrough book *Chez Nous* (2004), addresses the 1940s film star Rita Hayworth, who remarked (this is how Estes's poem begins):

> *I can never get a zipper*
> *to close. Maybe that stands*
> *for something, what do you think?*
> I think glamour is its own
> allure, thrashing and
> flashing, a lure, a spoon
> as in spooning, as in *l'amour*
> in Scotland, where I once watched
> the gorse-twisted hills unzip
> to let a cold blue lake
> between them.

The question mark that comes at the end of Hayworth's quotation introduces Estes's string of internally rhyming words; slow down there (or reread it very slowly) in order to make sure you hear the wordplay, the way that sounds migrate from word to word. "Glamour" in older English—or Scottish dialect—can also mean a spell, an illusion, a charm: the word *glamour* is (Estes continues)

> a Scottish variant
> of *grammar* with its rustle of moods
> and desires. Which brings us back to
> the zipper and why we want it
> to close, each hook climbing another
> the way words ascend a sentence, trying on
> its silver suture like clothes.

Estes makes her puns visible, suggesting that all allure is also a lure, that clothes, like poems, delight because they can both open and close. The uneven free-verse lines, breaking on unlikely words such as "to," close up or suture like zippers: language is sexier that way.

Balanced and delicate sonic patterns like Estes's can dazzle with self-conscious delight, imitating some fabulous part of the visible, tangible world. They can also work as counterpoint to the harsh, or disordered, or simply depressing situations outside a poem, inside a life. You can find a lot of those kinds of patterns—rhymed and otherwise—in the very compact poetry of Lorine Niedecker, who spent most of her life in the small lakeside town of Fort Atkinson, Wisconsin. Niedecker's mother apparently did not value her writing and could not hear well. Niedecker's memorial poems give her mother on paper, in sound, the richness that she could not have for most of her life, as if to show her, at last and quietly, what poetry could do:

> The branches' snow is like the cotton fluff
> she wore in her aching ears. In this deaf huff
> after storm shall we speak of love?
>
> As my absent father's distrait wife
> she worked for us—knew us by sight.
>
> We know her now by the way the snow
> protects the plants before they go.

The nonstandard spelling "distrait" means "distraught," but also perhaps "distracted" and "in dire straits": to these meanings and to Niedecker's end rhymes we can add the interplay of "snow" with "know" and "now," of "deaf" and "huff" and "wife." It is a chilly elegy—the snow protects some plants but freezes others—but an apt and, above all, an elegant one: rhyme caps the poem as snow caps reeds and leaves, as death in old age caps a frustrating life. We can read the poem for the family drama, for the characters Niedecker has sketched. But we can also savor the sadness, the elegance, the efficiency in the work that Niedecker makes each consonant do.

Not all displays of poetic technique attempt to make the poet stand out or get credit for beauty that seems exceptional. Sometimes—as with table manners or college admissions and standardized tests—technical competence, or technical excellence, shows that the poet belongs, or deserves to belong, to a group; it is a kind of demonstration, or else an audition, and the audition may be unfair.

We remember Phillis Wheatley (1753–1784; no relation to David) as the first African American poet to publish a book of poems, and the first widely noticed for her poetry (she was not the first to compose verse). But readers who come to her verse expecting the origins of a specifically Black, or specifically American, way of writing are sometimes surprised, even disappointed, to find that her poems sound and feel (at least at first) like thousands of other competent and more-than-competent poems by hundreds of poets from England. Most of them use what was by far the era's most common form, balanced and end-stopped rhymed couplets with ten syllables, alternating soft-loud, soft-loud, and so on, in each line:

> When first thy pencil did those beauties give,
> And breathing figures learnt from thee to live,
> How did those prospects give my soul delight,
> A new creation rushing on my sight?
> Still, wond'rous youth! each noble path pursue,
> On deathless glories fix thine ardent view:
> Still may the painter's and the poet's fire
> To aid thy pencil, and thy verse conspire!

These lines (whose meter is called iambic pentameter) come from Wheatley's "To S. M., a Young African Painter." They are praise that many beholders of that era, discovering many a young painter, might give, and they have the technical features you can find in many an eighteenth-century performance, with two nouns per line (in general), a breathing space (or caesura) midline, a clear and complete thought in every couplet, consistency in tone, elevated language, flawless regular meter.

But they mean something more because they describe an African painter—and because Wheatley wrote them. Given a serious classical education by the Boston matron who purchased her as a child, Phillis Wheatley flourished as a poet in her early teens, when Boston readers with abolitionist sympathies arranged to send her to London. Published in England, Wheatley's *Poems on Various Subjects* (1773) was not just a demonstration that she, an individual, could write in the era's accepted forms with confidence and skill, but also a demonstration that a dark-skinned, enslaved American of African origins could do so. The clear poetic technique that Wheatley had attained—prefiguring W. E. B. Du Bois's Talented Tenth a century later—was proof of concept for the idea that African Americans could do and learn and write anything that anyone else could, as well as having topics of their own.

Not all poetic forms rhyme, of course. Moreover, not all poetic forms are matters of soundplay, and not all are unique to poems. You already know how to make, and match, and recognize a written form if you have written a thank-you note, or a formal letter, or a five-paragraph AP essay, or a last will and testament. Each of these forms, like the sonnet or the eighteenth-century couplet, evokes particular expectations about what words and what kinds of language go where. And each of these prose forms can become a productive constraint or a template, whether for serious emulation or for sarcasm and distortion. Donne's scathing "The Will," for example, both imitates a last will and testament and parodies one, since he imagines himself as "dead" because a breakup has wrecked him. Here is the fifth of his six stanzas:

To him for whom the passing-bell next tolls,
I give my physic books; my written rolls
Of moral counsels I to Bedlam give;
My brazen medals unto them which live
In want of bread; to them which pass among
   All foreigners, mine English tongue:
     Though, Love, by making me love one
  Who thinks her friendship a fit portion
For younger lovers, dost my gifts thus disproportion.

"Physic" means "medicine"; "Bedlam" is a mental hospital. Donne gives each gift to people who cannot use it, just as he gave his own heart to someone who played him false and refused the gift. A literal, unironic will would be pointless, since nothing Donne owns has much value right now: that "one" whose "friendship" he has lost has made all his talents feel useless, all his worldly goods meaningless, leaving him with nothing he cares to give his friends (if he has any friends). The power in the poem lies in the relation between this parody will and a real one, in the ever-escalating, bitterer and bitterer absurdity of the clauses that make up Donne's verse bequest.

That will could not be legally executed, nor would any adult priest perform the tender mock catechism, the repetitive Christian-Sunday-school Q and A, of child and pet in William Blake's "The Lamb": "Little Lamb who made thee / Dost thou know who made thee? . . . Little Lamb I'll tell thee, / Little Lamb I'll tell thee!" Christ, the Lamb of God, made the actual lamb, as Christ also made the child. At least, so the child who speaks the poem believes. The catechistic poem, derived from actual catechisms, has acquired its own history and stands as its own formal challenge to poets later than Blake. Take Christina Rossetti's "Up-hill":

> Does the road wind up-hill all the way?
>   Yes, to the very end.
> Will the day's journey take the whole long day?
>   From morn to night, my friend.
>
> But is there for the night a resting-place?
>   A roof for when the slow dark hours begin.
> May not the darkness hide it from my face?
>   You cannot miss that inn.

Rossetti's conclusion, like Hughes's, hits hard; she has been asking, and answering, questions a child might have about adulthood and death, and she is giving the bleakest answers compatible with her variety of Christian belief. The whole of life is like climbing a hill, whatever the weather, all day. Life gets harder and harder until you die. There is no respite until death. The great thing about heaven, or perhaps just about death, is not that you get all your friends back or that you ride better roller coasters but that it finally supplies something like shelter or rest, as that long line about "slow dark hours" says (the attitude is not so far from Samuel Johnson's poem on Dr. Levet). And the hours—in heaven—will still feel dark and slow, as slow as the three stressed syllables that present them, shorter than the lines that ask the questions, shorter than the life they conclude.

These catechistic, Q-and-A-based forms survive into the twenty-first century; to recognize them *as* forms is to see

why they retain their power, and to notice how their force—
questions and answers, conclusion after conclusion, leading up
to one bigger conclusion—can work alongside their elegance.
Consider one of several poems that the twenty-first-century
poet Carrie Etter entitles "A Birthmother's Catechism":

How did you let him go?

With altruism, tears, and self-loathing

How did you let him go?

A nurse brought pills for drying up breast milk

How did you let him go?

Who hangs a birdhouse from a sapling?

Etter's book *Imagined Sons* concerns the real son whom
the poet, at seventeen, gave up for adoption; this poem (one of
several with the same title) plays on our expectations that the
questions we ask about our lives will change over time and
that they will have satisfying answers. For this birth mother,
neither expectation holds.

Patterns in poems, once you recognize their fulfillment—
with matching rhymes, repeated words, syntactic or semantic expectations met—can look like judgments rendered, like
questions answered, like the endings to stories you did not
know were being told. They can also look or feel like magic,
just as patterns outside the verbal arts, in dance, in song, in the
stars as seen by diviners, in the architecture of ancient temples,
can feel magical: they can seem to reflect a design built into

the poem, or the situation the poet describes, or the language, or the whole of the universe.

That does not mean all poets think they are casting spells. Some poets insist that craft is only craft, that they are no more (and maybe less) spiritually empowered than talented cabinet-makers and dressmakers. The patterns in their poems, these poets explain, do not reflect any purpose or shape in nature but rather help us handle the fact that nature and society have no clear shape, or none that can please us or fit us. The real world is a mess, the poem is neat, they're supposed to be different, and that's part of why we have poetry, part of why we might like neat forms. "What does it say over the door of Heaven," Richard Wilbur quips (in "For the New Railway Station in Rome"), "but *homo fecit* [a human being made it]?" Poets such as Wilbur and Estes use technical feats to celebrate "wit and wakefulness," intellect and consciousness, mastering what would otherwise be an unmasterable, scary world.

Other poets lean into the magic. The poet, gardener, mystic, and cookbook writer Ronald Johnson spent much of his life on a book-length poem called *ARK*, a one-hundred-segment work with no plot and no narrative. The pieces of *ARK*, which Johnson referred to as "beams" and "spires" (as if it were a cathedral), are at once a device for containing the sacred (like the Ark of the Covenant) and an emulation of Noah's ark. The best parts of *ARK* sound both ecstatic and compact, finding in the structure of language itself, in balanced sounds and parallel consonants, a happy hidden order in the world. Watching Fourth of July fireworks, which react now, in lights, to something that happened long ago, Johnson sees

years past
ladle fire forth
last air

all earth before
above belief
beyond compare

Johnson discovered these kinds of order, "nothing if not intricate," not only in sounds and in things that he saw but in letters, in the physical shapes of words. Perhaps the most often quoted "beam" begins with a set of visual puns that also suggest that this world is, after all, home:

eartheartheart
eartheartheart
eartheartheart
eartheartheart
eartheartheart
eartheartheart

The earth is also our hearth, the heart of our art, if only our ear could hear all that art. You can read Johnson's orthographic grid as spelling out "earth, ear, the art, hear the art, heart," or as containing other similar messages, not so much put there by the poet as revealed, like spirits that were always there.

The scholar Herbert Tucker agrees with Johnson, claiming that poetry in general works like magic. Poets (Tucker says) take words beyond "reason's historically lengthening reach" on a "self-appointed mission to articulate the ineffable and say what can't be said." Such poets want to show what it's like to be in the grip of a mystery, to cast—or else to fall under—a spell. You can find poets whose elaborate music fits their experience of that spell. John Keats's "Ode to a Nightingale" begins as the nightingale's song sends Keats into a swoon or a hallucination or a vision, or perhaps he swooned first and then heard the song:

> My heart aches, and a drowsy numbness pains
>> My sense, as though of hemlock I had drunk,
> Or emptied some dull opiate to the drains
>> One minute past, and Lethe-wards had sunk:
> 'Tis not through envy of thy happy lot,
>> But being too happy in thine happiness,—
>>> That thou, light-winged Dryad of the trees,
>>>> In some melodious plot
> Of beechen green, and shadows numberless,
>> Singest of summer in full-throated ease.

A dryad is a wood nymph or forest fairy; Lethe is the mythological river whose water makes dead spirits forget their past lives. Keats is collapsing, feeling transported elsewhere, through his excessive identification with the "happiness" of the nightingale, whose song—manifest in Keats's elaborate stanza—transports him to a paradisal underworld. Song is a kind of trigger for emotions so deep that he cannot give them visual form, though he can imagine, by "happy" contrast, the space where the nightingale lives, the space full of luscious "ease" ("trees," "beechen green") that he prefers to his own head.

Keats has some goals in common with other terrific poets of flaunted technique, from George Herbert to Angie Estes, and other goals and effects in common with (say) the author and the fans of *The Lord of the Rings*. He's interested in magic and escape. As Keats pursues that song through his six stanzas, he finds that its pleasures cannot stay with him forever, that he is going to return to his own life and to human history, where individuals and societies change, even though the nightingale's song stays the same. (Keats later compares himself to the biblical figure Ruth, who left her birth society for good, and perhaps missed it: "She stood in tears amid the alien corn," that is, foreign wheat.)

To read this kind of poetry—this elaborate, lush, self-conscious, enchanting kind—with pleasure is to get almost lost in its elaborateness, as in a greenhouse or a botanic garden. This particular poem spells out, takes pains to acknowledge, our wish for magic, our wish to escape, but also the impossibility of a total escape: we exist in time and breathe air on earth, where we need to eat (if not to eat wheat). We cannot live only and always in a mysterious, magical, unseen other world. But we can take poetic elaboration as a way to imagine we do, or else to pay an extended visit.

Keats's stanza may seem today both beautiful and antique: few contemporary poets would attempt to duplicate it exactly. The modern US poets most invested in magic (Ronald Johnson among them) are those least likely to copy the English past. If you read only a little present-day poetry, you may wonder whether most of the forms of the past have fallen into disuse. If you read a lot of it, though, you can find almost all of those forms somewhere, many of them in excellent shape.

Learning to like more versions of pattern and form—and getting excited about what poets can do with those forms—means learning to recognize forms that come from outside poetry, like the last will and testament or the Q and A. It also means learning to recognize some forms' old rules.

The most recognizable, most frequent old form in English is the sonnet; we have already seen a few, in parts or complete. A standard sonnet has fourteen lines, usually divided (by sense or by rhyme scheme) into groups of eight and six or four, four, four, and two, usually in ten-syllable lines, with rhymes. Shakespeare wrote 154 of them, almost all rhymed *abab cdcd efef gg*; there have been sonnets with all sorts of rhyme schemes, or with none, in almost every generation since. To write sonnets, or to use any other old form, is to acknowledge your membership in a long-term community. No recent writer of sonnets can pretend to be the first. As with all traditional forms, though, writers can treat sonnets' history ironically or sarcastically, as well as reverently or gingerly. They can even play with those forms and their constraints without *using* them at all. In Catherynne Valente's terrific fantasy novel *The Girl Who Soared over Fairyland and Cut the Moon in Two*, the heroine meets two circus performers whose bodies are made of paper:

> "Oh, forgive us, of course we don't know you yet," said the boy, whose long, tall body was covered in blocks of text, little birthmarks of fourteen lines each. He was made of sonnets, from head to toe. His hair was a flutter of motley ribbon marks. An intricate origami looked September in the eye, folded and smoothed and peaked into a friendly, narrow face.

"But we feel as though we do!" cried the girl, whose body was the warm, expensive gold of old letters, an elegant calligraphy covering every inch of her round, excited cheeks, her acrobat's costume, her long, red, sealing-wax hair. . . . "I'm Valentine," she said, holding out her angular hand.

"I'm Pentameter," said the sonnet boy. "We're them." Both Valentine and Pentameter pointed their thumbs over their shoulders at a vivid sign, nailed to the pole that hoisted up the trapeze platforms. In deep scarlet it read: AEROPOSTE: WINGED WORDS AND FLIGHTS OF FANCY! Small golden wings flapped at the edges of the letters, the tail of the Y, the bar of the T. . . .

Pentameter grinned. Silky, blackly inked words formed his top lip: *For thy sweet love remember'd such wealth brings.* The cursive line of his bottom, smiling lip curved to finish the couplet: *That then I scorn to change my state with kings.*

Those italic lines conclude Shakespeare's Sonnet 29, "When in disgrace with fortune and men's eyes." If that were your first encounter with the term *sonnet*—as for many of Valente's readers it is—what would you have learned about sonnets? They have a history that includes friendship and love; they are playful but also formal; they represent the union of pentameters and valentines, old metrical forms and romantic or erotic attraction. They do tricks; they've been doing tricks—showing formal skill, like trapeze artists—for a long time, but they can still seem fresh and young. Reading sonnets, Valente suggests, is like watching acrobats. And they are fun to learn to watch, especially when you are just starting out as a serious reader (Valente's heroine is thirteen).

What do you do with a sonnet after you can recognize it, after you have learned to use the form, after you've learned to recognize that history? Individual writers of sonnets can defend the form in verse, and many have (Wordsworth even wrote an unsubtle sonnet that begins "Scorn not the sonnet," adding "with this key / Shakespeare unlocked his heart"). But writers of sonnets can also attack the sonnet form and its prominent, privileged history. Terrance Hayes has taken up—or taken down—the sonnet sporadically throughout his career, most famously with a tour de force called "Sonnet" in *Hip Logic* (2002); the poem comprises fourteen repetitions of the same line, "We cut the watermelon into smiles." Hayes's fourteen iterations play on racist stereotypes that associate rural Black Americans with watermelon and fixed grins, and on the assumption that all sonnets say or mean the same thing. Hayes brings to mind the old schoolroom punishment whereby disobedient children were made to write the same line over and over, as if these kinds of insincere repetitions are what we have learned to expect from one another, or from sonnets, or from Black poets, or from him. And he points back to another poem in another challenging form, the African American writer Paul Laurence Dunbar's famous stanzaic lyric of 1895: "We wear the mask that grins and lies."

Hayes in 2018 published an entire collection of sonnets, each of which has the same title: "American Sonnet for My Past and Future Assassin." Its fourteen-line projects react to the poet's own frustration with his fame (which eats up his time with worthy obligations, isolates him, and cannot give him peace), as well as reacting fiercely to America under Trump. Hayes's "American Sonnets" also replace conventional rhyme schemes with much denser sonic arrangements, often untethered to line ends. One of them insults a critic "who cannot distinguish a blackbird from a raven": "You don't know how / To describe your own face. In the mirror you coo / Gibberish where the shape of your mouth escapes you." Another sonnet lets loose on politicians whose words are all lies or meaningless sounds: "Junk country, stump speech. The umpteenth boast / Stumps our toe. The umpteenth falsehood stumps / Our elbows & eyeballs, our Nos, Whoas, wows, woes." The cascade of open vowels, the almost show-offy feel in these repetitions (Hayes uses the word "umpteenth" eight times in fourteen lines) suggest a fed-up citizen, and also a writer whose expertise with words adds to his moral authority: somebody who can write like that knows, if anybody knows, what words can do.

Modern sonnets (Hayes's included) almost all have the same number of lines: you know, once you start one of them, about where it'll end, though you may have no clue how the poet will get there. Other fixed forms create stanzas, building blocks, for poems that can take any length; the challenge, the technical accomplishment, shows up in how the poet can reuse but vary the stanza form within a given poem. Near the end of the first part of his comic narrative *Don Juan* (1819), Lord Byron, or his narrator, tells us what kind of story he means to tell:

My poem's epic, and is meant to be
    Divided in twelve books; each book containing,
With love, and war, a heavy gale at sea,
    A list of ships, and captains, and kings reigning,
New characters; the episodes are three:
    A panoramic view of Hell's in training,
After the style of Virgil and of Homer,
So that my name of Epic's no misnomer.

"Homer"-"misnomer": Byron uses the stanza (called *ottava rima*, "eight-rhyme" in Italian) to explain his "epic" verse form. But Byron is kidding: his playful and in part satirical intention comes out in the rhymes, which show us a man who is having fun, who cares for the sounds of the language he is assembling, for the stanza as an assemblage of sounds, far more than he can care (or make us care) for the "captains, and kings," the loves and the wars, he presents. Byron's most famous rhymes are—not by coincidence—polysyllabic: this kind of rhyme lends itself to stunt-like or comic effects. (Polysyllabic rhyme used to be called "feminine rhyme," while monosyllabic rhymes, like "boat" and "coat," were "masculine.")

You can enjoy hearing a form used well in familiar ways or watching one poet use it over and over expertly: *Don Juan* will give you hundreds of examples of over-the-top, extravagant, humorous rhyming (the most famous being "intellectual" with "hen pecked you all"). You can also enjoy seeing a poet wrench a form out of its familiar groove to make it do something quite new. Ottava rima in English, which tends to move fast and to highlight all its rhymes, almost always got used for narrative or comedy, or both, until W. B. Yeats realized that he had the chops to make it serious and reflective:

> We too had many pretty toys when young;
> A law indifferent to blame or praise,
> To bribe, or threat; habits that made old wrong
> Melt down, as it were wax in the sun's rays;
> Public opinion ripening for so long
> We thought it would outlive all future days.
> O what fine thoughts we had because we thought
> That the worst rogues and rascals had died out.

This stanza ended up in the poem Yeats first called "Thoughts upon the Present State of the World" (the final version has the title "Nineteen Hundred and Nineteen" instead): it reacts to the carnage of World War I and the Anglo-Irish War. It's a stanza whose rhymes have force—you can't ignore them—but also one where they do not show off. Byron flaunted his rhymes; Yeats hides most of them, then highlights "thought" and "out." What pops out instead as signs of his indignation are changes in what kinds of words he can use: the calm, optimistic liberal past is Latinate and lengthy ("public opinion ripening"); the present, when things have gone to hell, takes monosyllables: ("fine thoughts," "the worst," "died out").

Yeats wrote in an earlier poem, "Adam's Curse," that verse technique—like cosmetics—ought to make its labor invisible: "A line will take us hours maybe / Yet if it does not seem a moment's thought / All our stitching and unstitching has been nought." But Yeats did not always want us to see the stitchings of rhyme, or any other part of verse technique, as natural, effortless, mostly concealed. Sometimes he wanted to show us that it could take work. That's part of another Yeats tour de force, "The Fascination of What's Difficult." Here is the whole poem, first published in 1910, when Yeats was in the thick of managing a controversial Dublin theater:

The fascination of what's difficult
Has dried the sap out of my veins, and rent
Spontaneous joy and natural content
Out of my heart. There's something ails our colt
That must, as if it had not holy blood
Nor on Olympus leaped from cloud to cloud,
Shiver under the lash, strain, sweat and jolt
As though it dragged road-metal. My curse on plays
That have to be set up in fifty ways,
On the day's war with every knave and dolt,
Theatre business, management of men.
I swear before the dawn comes round again
I'll find the stable and pull out the bolt.

At the Abbey Theater (which he cofounded), Yeats had to sit on committees, approve plays, manage budgets, hire directors, supervise set designers and costumers, take part in publicity campaigns, and generally do everything but write the poetry that had made him famous enough to take this sort of job. You can read the poem as Yeats's weary protest against what is now called (after a 1969 business book) the Peter Principle: if you are good enough at your job, you will be promoted again and again until you wind up in a job that does not suit you.

You can also read it as a poem about kinds of work, and about visible and invisible, pleasurable and simply draining, technique. "Theater business" had proven difficult in one way because he had to deal with difficult people (actors, for example); writing thirteen lines rhyming *abb acc add aeea* proved difficult in another, but Yeats can accomplish the latter with vigor, even with a sardonic glee that the poem invites you to share. The poem looks like (but is not) a sonnet and does not change its apparent subject, nor its key rhyme, in the middle, as a sonnet would. (Helen Vendler, in her persuasive book on Yeats's forms, hears an "implied sonnet-structure," an "absent fourteenth line," and a dig at the European continent, since Pegasus, originally Greek, "is now stabled in Ireland.")

Yeats's scheme also resembles another Italian form, the terza rima of Dante's *Divine Comedy*, *aba bcb cdc ded*, whose appearance in English almost always suggests Dante's journey through purgatory or hell. (We saw a small slice of this form already in P. B. Shelley's "Ode to the West Wind.") Except that Yeats doesn't exactly use terza rima, just as he doesn't exactly write a sonnet: rather than rhyming *aba bcb cdc*, he keeps coming back to the *a* rhyme ("difficult," "colt," "bolt"). Being a theater manager is like a taking journey through hell, the terza rima element implies, except that you never get anywhere. Yeats's insistent, muscular repetition—that "ult"-"olt" sound keeps coming back when you thought you were done with it—mimics the insistence on finance, on "business," on "management of men," that Yeats tried hard (so the poem says) to see as a challenge rather than as an impediment. Running a theater company made the poet's wheels spin; it ground down his moving parts; it made the very blood drain from his body—so he imagined, figuring blood as sap, himself as a tree. It also hobbled a horse, and not just any horse but the Muses' winged horse, Pegasus, who has to "drag." Having introduced these figures, Yeats can move on to his literal complaint—being a manager sucks!—and then return to his figures and find a solution: he'll quit (he does not really quit), or at least swear a lot about quitting (he does that here). "I swear" (most middle managers swear) "I'll find the stable and pull out the bolt," both releasing the winged horse from its bondage and making further work, further drudgery, impossible.

Terza rima makes a good example, not just of a form that provides a challenge, but also of a form that shows the difference between one language and another: taking pleasure in how a poem uses this form means noticing and taking pleasure in the affordances of a particular language. Most modern poets who translate Dante (there have been dozens) find his terza rima a bridge too far: one of them, John Ciardi, writes that "in Italian, where it is only a slight exaggeration to say that everything rhymes with everything else . . . the rhyme is no problem; in English it is a disaster." In short poems designed for the English language, though, terza rima can be less a disaster than a high-difficulty maneuver, a steep challenge. Yeats himself accepted the challenge in what seems to have been the last poem he wrote, and the only one fully in Dante's form.

Like "The Fascination of What's Difficult," this last poem imagines a very talented man asked to do something he will find far from congenial. But Yeats's "Cuchulain Comforted" refuses to celebrate poetry, nobility, aloofness, violence, or even exceptional skill, instead seeking the opposite of power, the opposite of a noble (or manly) victory, in line with Yeats's reflections on his own humbling old age. The dead Irish

hero and warrior-king Cuchulain finds himself in the afterlife among "bird-like things," though they do not fly. One of
them tells him, in the last half of the poem, that he should join
the bird-creatures and "make a shroud":

> "Now we shall sing and sing the best we can,
> But first you must be told our character:
> Convicted cowards all, by kindred slain
>
> "Or driven from home and left to die in fear."
> They sang, but had nor human tunes nor words,
> Though all was done in common as before,
>
> They had changed their throats and had the throats of birds.

These bird-cowards, forever weaving, calmly grieving,
and working only as a group, must be the opposite of the
individualistic, brooding, martial, more-than-human king.
Words echo or "become" other words through the intricacies
of Yeats's craft, too, over and above those rhymes: "kindred"
leads to "human," "home" to "human" again, "human" to
"common." The quiet terza rima, recommending a craft that
amounts to resignation, a way to see beyond ambition, fits
what are almost literally Yeats's last written words.

Dante might have expected later poets to adapt his terza
rima in order to write about the afterlife, but he could not have
anticipated "Ode to the West Wind" or "Cuchulain Comforted." Nor could he have expected Hayes's combination of
terza rima and the cadences of the blues in Hayes's poem
"The Blue Terrance." The right poet can adapt the hoariest,
most traditional forms to make them contemporary and especially responsive to people, places, or experiences Renaissance

Italy could not have known. You can track those adaptations through almost any old European form that remains in use today. That's what the terrific British poet Patience Agbabi has done with the difficult thirty-nine-line form called the sestina in her 2000 volume *Transformatrix*. "Give me a stage and I'll cut form on it," Agbabi declares; "give me a page and I'll perform on it." Agbabi (and she is hardly the only one) finds cadences and topics from modern performance poetry fully compatible with Yeats's or Shakespeare's forms. Her volume holds seven sestinas, including one about a girl named Leila ("night" in Hebrew and Arabic) who

> controls the dark . . .
> as if she were princess of the dark
> eclipsing the prince, wrapping a century of time
> round her ring finger.

The same exceptional book includes a Nigerian Afro-futurist manifesto, "UFO Woman (Pronounced Oofoe)," and a monologue in Nigerian-British immigrant English ("The Wife of Bafa"), the first among Agbabi's many adaptations of Chaucer's *Canterbury Tales*.

More recherché forms than the sonnet or even the sestina lend themselves to this kind of renewal, the kind that can make you marvel not just at what a new poet has done with a form but at how that poet has given it a moral charge far removed from its (white or European) origins. The canzone is a very challenging form from medieval Provence whose eleven-line stanzas repeat a small number of end words. The one at the beginning of Reginald Dwayne Betts's *Bastards of the Reagan Era* follows all the Provençal rules. Yet Betts's

2013 poem (with its metrics indebted partly to the older US poet Yusef Komunyakaa, partly to the trochaic irregularities of hip-hop) could not have been written much earlier than it was:

> The black
> hole is now the block. Steel
> swallows men, spits them out black
> eyed, spits them out black-
> balled. Reagan's curse might be real
> might be what has niggas black-
> mailing themselves, dancing in black
> face. Chocolate city red
> under the scrutiny. Asphalt red.

"Chocolate city" is a vernacular nickname for the majority–African American city of Washington, DC. Betts is bringing the European form to his own city, in his and its toughest hour.

Then there are formal challenges in modern English—verse patterns that can make you say "Oh!" or "Aha!"—whose forms were not European to begin with. The word *ghazal*, when it first appeared, described a genre in classical Arabic, a kind of love poem in monorhyme; only once it was brought to another Islamic culture and another language, Persian, did the word come to mean a fixed form, with syntactically independent couplets (each one makes sense on its own), a rhyme before each couplet's repeated final word or phrase, and the poet's name or pseudonym somewhere in the final couplet. Rumi, among others, excelled in these ghazals. Urdu ghazals were and still are frequently sung. During the late 1960s, partly in homage to the Urdu poet Mirza Ghalib, the already-eminent US poet Adrienne Rich started writing poems that she labeled ghazals, whose two-line stanzas jumped from topic to topic, as the literal English translations of Ghalib's had done. She did not, though, follow the Persian-Urdu rules. Other poets writing in English created free-verse ghazals along Rich's lines for about thirty years.

Then the Kashmiri American poet Agha Shahid Ali got irked. He had grown up knowing the form in Urdu and had translated Ghalib himself; by the late 1990s he wanted to show Americans what the form could do. His attempt made the story of the ghazal in America into a good example of how poets and readers learn to appreciate, and seek, and excel in, a form that's quite old but feels new. During the last five years of his life, Ali assembled a series of polemical essays; an anthology of "real ghazals" by many hands, *Ravishing DisUnities*; and an entire book, *Call Me Ishmael Tonight* (2002), consisting entirely of his own ghazals in the strict Persian-Urdu form.

These ghazals take up Ali's own continuing subjects: the militarized destruction of his native Kashmir, his friendships with other American poets, his immersion in several cultures' legends (especially Islam, though he was no orthodox believer), his strong and sometimes erotic attachments to friends, his sense of having lost his home. The ghazals also, with their rhymes on unstressed syllables (such as "into" with "slew"), act out a fluent, South Asian–inflected English that is rarely what monoglot Americans expect:

I took the shortest route through Belief's sad country
when archangels, on the Word's command, slew my word. . . .

Forgive me, please; could we be alone forever?

I have never been alone; I'll live to rue my word. . . .

Yours too, Shahid, will be a radical departure.
You'll go out of yourself and then into my word.

You can see ghazals, almost as you can see sonnets, in
many collections today, written to varying degrees of for-
mality and with varying senses of what the form has meant,
but always with some sense that it's an accomplishment, that
making a ghazal work is, well, *work,* as well as play, adapting
with pleasure to a constraint. Tarfia Faizullah's "Self-Portrait
as Mango" (another self-portrait, like those in chapter 2) uses
the ghazal to hit back hard against ethnic stereotypes about
Asian Americans. The repeated image and the repeated word
pick up her insistence and her anger, and also link her back to
the form's geographic origins:

She says, *Your English is great! How long have you been in our*
    country?
I say, *Suck on a mango, bitch, since that's all you think I eat anyway.*
    Mangoes.

are what margins like me know everything about, right?
    Doesn't
a mango just win spelling bees and kiss white boys? Isn't a
    mango

a placeholder in a poem folded with burkas? But this one,
the one I'm going to slice and serve down her throat, is a
    mango

that remembers jungles jagged with insects, the river's darker
    thirst.

Faizullah's snarky ghazal, with its stack of rejected stereotypes, makes a good example of what the poet Monica Youn calls proleptic form, form as a kind of defense against accusations or assumptions that the poet has come to expect and wants to fend off; in this case, the assumption that a visibly South Asian person would feel less at home in English, or less American, or less entitled to write poems, than writers with paler skin. The repeated word "mango" also attacks the idea that South Asians, or people from Islamic cultures, are somehow all alike, as similar as the mangos in a box. Faizullah's sense of who she is and has been (not to mention her way with sarcasm) makes her stronger and more verbally adept than the casually racist questioner would expect. Her ghazal breaks some "real ghazal" rules, since the sense runs on from couplet to couplet (traditional ghazal couplets must be self-contained) and the couplets use no rhyme, just the repeated titular word.

The ghazal is not the only distinguished, old, non-European form that American poets have made their own. Haiku may seem like a zone for beginners now, yet Tonya Foster's magnificent if sometimes befuddling *A Swarm of Bees in High Court* (2015) feels like the long-delayed American apotheosis of haiku form. She does not write fully traditional haiku (freestanding, improvisational, about the seasons). Instead, much of her book uses the shape of the haiku (normally, three lines of, respectively, five, seven, and five syllables) as an approximate stanza. Any page, any poem, any stanza could stand on its own or join some larger, nonnarrative unit: "As if the soul could / be singled out from the cells, / from the room's clutter."

Such interlocking forms fit Foster's sense of a New York City in which everything is connected, pollination and gentrification and cocktail recipes and hate and love: "red as distant Red Hook bees drunk on cherry fungicide cocktails, / red as distant space mapped bought and belonging to brutish say-so." ("Red Hook," here, refers to the neighborhood in Brooklyn; each line's sixteen syllables are almost, but not quite, the size of a haiku.) Windows that overlook windows resemble the poet who wants to look out on everything, to be Henry James's proverbial ideal writer, on whom nothing is lost:

> To see and to be
> seen is what it is to live on
> perennial blocks;
>
> to see and to be
> seen as somehow familiar
> with all the look-backs.

Almost everything in Foster's ambiguous lingo ("blocks," for instance) could be a pun—it all signifies twice. Foster's verse units can be disassembled and reassembled, like Legos—they portray a city in manifold ambiguities rather than telling one big story. They can also tell small stories, two per page:

> He's asleep
> after telling her about the boy
> he was, his father's fists.
>
> He's a sleep
> she can't fall to, a nap that
> won't keep or unkink.

Like Langston Hughes, Foster knows that Harlem is both a place where people live and a symbol for Black America, whether or not its residents want it that way: "Harlem, she can't / get tour buses of eyes to stop / trailing through her thoughts." And like Hughes, Foster understands that economics underpin and constrain emotion, even for children who just want to play: "Blackity black girl, / at play on the court of (y)our skin— / eminent domain." If you are looking for a book whose terrific technique uses very old forms in new ways and you would prefer a form that is not deeply, historically European or white, it's hard to overstate how valuable Foster's book might be for you, how much new interest it can bring to an old—and already international, cross-cultural—constraint.

I have been showing how poets adopt inherited constraints, play with them, and give pleasure by making old rules seem new. Many of us got the impression in school, especially if we are over (say) thirty, that poets had to choose between traditional constraints, forms, rules (whether Western or non-Western) and something called free verse, which had no rules; we were told, as well, to associate the modern with the frame-breaking, the apparently revolutionary, the entirely new.

To misquote Luke Skywalker in *Star Wars: The Last Jedi*: almost every word in that sentence was wrong. We live in a moment when new forms are flourishing, and by "flourishing" I mean they seem to be everywhere, and by "new" I mean truly made up, by one person or by a group of named individuals, during the twentieth or the twenty-first century. One of the most discussed (and best-selling) poems in modern Canada is Christian Bök's collection of prose poems, *Eunoia*. Here are a few sentences from "Chapter E":

Enfettered, these sentences repress free speech. The text deletes selected letters.... Relentless, the rebel peddles these theses, even when vexed peers deem the precepts "mere dreck." The plebes resent newer verse; nevertheless, the rebel perseveres, never deterred, never dejected, heedless, even when hecklers heckle the vehement speeches. We feel perplexed whenever we see these excerpted sentences. We sneer when we detect the clever scheme—the emergent repetend: the letter E. We jeer; we jest.

Bök's literary "rebel" uses the literary form called the lipogram, in which the writer avoids one or more letters—here, all vowels except "e." ("Chapter A" uses only "a," and so on.) It's a technique invented for fun, for showing off, and it resembles a mathematical game more than it resembles the kinds of techniques (such as Yeats's rhyme) that can ever sound natural in English.

Lipograms came to Canada and the US from the mostly French group of writers called OULIPO ("Workshop for Potential Literature," in French: *Ouvroir de littérature potentielle*) along with such other math-y forms as the snowball, with its incrementally increasing number of words or syllables, one in the first line, two in the second, five in the fifth:

sun
you stun
with your gun
aimed at no one

sol
crisol

o frijol
grito bemol.

These bilingual examples (the Spanish—not a translation—
means "sun / melting pot / or bean / flat scream") come
from Urayoán Noel, who also uses that other OULIPO device, the chain of anagrams, in his poem "UNITED STATES /
ESTADOS UNIDOS":

STEADIEST NUT

SEDATED UNITS

SAUTEED TINTS. . . .

OSO DESNUDISTA

NUDISTA SEDOSO

TISÚS ONDEADOS

SUDANTE SIDOSO

(The last four lines in English: "stripper bear / silky nudist /
wavy tissues / sweaty person with AIDS"). Not only the idea
of the United States but the very words used to create it feel
different, Noel suggests, in different languages.

The original OULIPO writers, among them the novelist
Italo Calvino, wanted to make literature that felt less like a tradition and more like a game; their programs, or inventions, or
stunts, have appealed to American poets, Noel among them,
for serious purposes. Cathy Park Hong put the lipogram to
strongly political use with her parable of the Western frontier,
"Ballad in O"; in that poem "bold cowboys lock horns, /
forlorn hobos plot to rob // pots of gold, loco mobs drool for
blood," and all of them "throng / to hood crooks to strong
wood posts." The distance and alienation, the cooling-off

effect, created by all the *o*'s allows Hong to focus in, slowly, on what turns out to be an Old West lynch mob.

Such forms have a high neat quotient or shock value: *Somebody wrote a poem with just one vowel! How cool is that? Can I do it too?* Over and above those responses, though, OULIPO forms, and similar forms that flaunt their recency and artificiality, have uses that sonnets, for example, cannot. We have seen how subdued rhymes, and fluently metrical stanzas, and orthographic puns (like Ronald Johnson's "earth"-"hearth") can seem to celebrate, or at least to affirm, some power already there in the language itself: poets simply harness it naturally, like windmills, or dig it right out of the soil, like miners in a gold rush. OULIPO forms such as lipograms look, conversely, like something we do to and with the language, not like something we find already, naturally, there—they are inevitably, consciously artificial. Those forms can have special appeal for poets who want us to question whatever we have seen as natural, to ask whether the forms of school, of the workplace, of the family, might be artificial and changeable as well.

Other impressive forms postdate the OULIPO group; living poets invented them, and recently. Some of those forms depend on technology, as in Cortney Lamar Charleston's "Spell Check Questions the Validity of Black Life," where smartphones misunderstand—as white society misunderstands—Black Lives Matter. Each of Charleston's stanzas begins with a smartphone's mistaken "correction" for the name of a Black American killed by white men with guns or by police:

[Trayvon] Martin: did you mean traction?
Yes, in the way that lynching, the first
quintessential American sport, has regained its
footing among a younger generation—no robes
worn, no fouls given, not a whistle to blow.

Until recently (the form has other exponents now) nobody
had written a smartphone-autocorrect poem, about Black Lives
Matter or about anything else. Other invented forms, such as
the Golden Shovel, have caught on fast. Terrance Hayes introduced the Golden Shovel with two poems in his 2010 volume
Lighthead. A Golden Shovel takes all its line-ending words from
a poem (any poem) by Gwendolyn Brooks, the great midcen-
tury poet of Black Chicago; the poem therefore has as many
lines as the source from Brooks has words. Hayes's first Golden
Shovel, called "The Golden Shovel," takes its line ends from
Brooks's often-reproduced poem "We Real Cool" and its title
from Brooks's subtitle, "Seven at the Golden Shovel" (i.e., seven
teens hanging out at a pool hall). Hayes offers Brooks's cultural
and poetic inheritance as a kind of welcome substitute for a
more difficult literal family and its literal inheritance:

When I am so small Da's sock covers my arm, we
cruise at twilight until we find the place the real

men lean, bloodshot and translucent with cool.
His smile is a gold-plated incantation as we

drift by women on bar stools, with nothing left
in them but approachlessness. This is a school

I do not know yet.

Not the bar, not the birth family or families, not the pool hall described in Brooks's poem "We Real Cool," but Brooks's poetry is the superior "school." The Chicago high school teacher Peter Kahn helped to popularize the Golden Shovel after other poets had taken it up; Kahn coedited a massive and much-noticed 2017 anthology of Golden Shovels, with examples by many, many senior poets alongside high school students attracted to that form, that "school."

Another Hayesian form comes from newspapers' word puzzles. Poems with this template, from Hayes's *Hip Logic* (2002), use, as line endings, only words formed from the letters in a one-word title (the title "hedgehog" could generate, as permissible line-ending words, "edge," "heed," "God"). As with the lipogram, a form whose rules make it sound frivolous or arbitrary can turn serious quite fast. One of Hayes's anagram poems, "segregate," follows "a young tree / frog" who just wants to go to school:

> The girls are eager to transform him with a kiss; the boys
>   eager
> to see him on the basketball court. But the principal greets
> him with a "Get the Hell out of here!" A security guard
>   fetches the tear
> gas. Some of the older teachers crowd in the doorway like
>   befuddled geese.
> "You belong in our swamps not our schools!" they rage.
> But clearly the cool-blooded Amphibian-American does
>   not agree.

It's a stunt or a joke about frogs and princes, and it is, of course, more than a joke about desegregation, about how frustrating it must be for those who try to change racist systems over-night, how it feels to go first, how pioneers of desegregation are often told, or required, to stay "cool-blooded" while those around them heat up. You can see all those implications in Hayes's poem before, or after, you admire the ingenuity of the form.

Other poets accept that form's challenge too. Monica Youn's *Blackacre* (2016) includes a poem called "Testament of the Hanged Man"; it imagines a man dismembered, strung out and separated into parts:

> Item: a man
> now pendant (still sen-
> tient), as tempted, as
> amen—
>
> able as Odysseus, strapped to the mast,
> seeking knowledge sans
> experience: a test
> (or a tease).

Youn's end words use only the letters in "testament" as they testify to alienation and its "seam- / less unseen net"; her constraint collapses into rigorous pentameters by the end of the poem, announcing "I bequeath this mean estate / to whoever hungers to taste this marbled meat." Youn's poem about self-hatred, about how it feels to distance oneself from one's own desires, also looks back (as do other poems in *Blackacre*) to the medieval French poet and thief François Villon's autobiographical verse *Testament*. Satisfying multiple for-mal constraints—anagrams, short stanza forms, a pentameter quatrain—Youn also fits the requirements of the poetic last will and testament, like Donne's "The Will." As in many of Youn's poems, the difficulty, the emotional stress and strain, of satisfying so many constraints, meeting so many imposed or inherited requirements, becomes itself one of the feelings that the poem includes.

I'll end this chapter with the pleasures, the formal requirements, the virtuoso arrangements, in one more modern poet's invented forms, which also chip and chisel novel pleasures out of strict, and apparently arbitrary, constraints. Again, they are forms we can follow into our own time (in a passel of poets, from Angie Estes to David Baker), though here I'll stick to examples from one poet's work. About half of Marianne Moore's best poems use syllabics (lines that count syllables rather than beats or metrical feet) alongside rhyme. The resulting stanzas, whose lines often break or rhyme on words like "of" or "an," can seem fractured, or jagged, or like a counterintuitive pattern imposed (as if by a scientific model) over a world whose underlying rules do not match up with our intuitions. You have to learn patience, to look more closely than usual, to see what rules really apply.

One of Moore's first great triumphs in this way of writing is "The Fish" (1918). As in many of Moore's poems, the title begins a sentence that continues into the body text:

The Fish

wade
through black jade.

Of the crow-blue mussel shells, one keeps
    adjusting the ash-heaps,
       opening and shutting itself like

an
injured fan.
    The barnacles which encrust the side
    of the wave, cannot hide
       there, for the submerged shafts of the

sun,
split like spun
    glass, move themselves with spotlight swiftness
    into the crevices—

These lines, with their breaks on "the" and "an," seem sliced up in a way that might strike you as new, whether or not you have noticed the way that they repeat their syllable counts: each full stanza has lines of one, three, eleven, six, and eight syllables. To carry off eight stanzas in this mode (and some of Moore's syllabic rhymed stanzas are far more elaborate) is itself an achievement; her modernist peers, such as Ezra Pound and T. S. Eliot, recognized its originality.

Moore's noun phrases fit the imagined ocean around and below the shafts of sunlight on the waves. They're beautiful, certainly, but they are also "injured," consistently broken up in ways that suggest fresh damage. That damage, associated later with "iron," with ships that have sunk (Moore could be describing a sunken ship), with "external / marks of abuse," also marks "The Fish" as a poem of response to catastrophe, even of naval warfare, interested in damaged beauty and in the damage that sunken ships represent. The poem gets overtly violent as it continues; the "chasm-side," we learn, "is dead" and has seen some sort of devastation, perhaps an undersea earthquake. Moore's brother John was a naval chaplain during the First World War; the poem may also consider the danger he faced, and certainly its colors and highlights try hard to show us at once a beautiful and various undersea world and a damaged world, a world at war.

Moore's displays of technical bravura, her language made intricate as if for its own sake, are also ways to celebrate self-protection, ironically or wholeheartedly, as if each trill in a baroque sonata or each flourish in a metal guitar solo were an expression of trust or a victory over fear. You can find that kind of trust, and that kind of complexity, in one of Moore's most overtly beautiful stanzaic poems, "The Paper Nautilus," with its opening blast against (overwhelmingly male) "commuters" who expect "teatime comforts" from their wives. Soon the poem morphs into Moore's overt tribute to mothers (including her own), to all the underacknowledged work, all the effortful protection, given to children by mothers and mother figures. In the last half of Moore's 1940 poem, "it" is the titular nautilus, whose

> eggs coming from
> the shell free it when they are freed—
> leaving its wasp-nest flaws
> of white-on-white, and close-

> laid Ionic chiton-folds
> like the lines in the mane of
> a Parthenon horse,

round which the arms had
wound themselves as if they know love
    is the only fortress
    strong enough to trust to.

That's the end of the poem. The whole thing has five stanzas with recurring rhymes, among them "succeed" with "freed" and "of" with "love." But the poem's sense of closure, of finality, of something accomplished, does not depend on rhyme: the last line stands without one. Moore relies instead on syntax, on a network of clauses that interact and build on one another almost like the successive chambers and egg sacs of the nautilus, an animal that works so hard, like many human mothers, on something to which she has given birth, something she must protect, and something that will ultimately—if she has done everything right—leave her behind.

Moore's lines wrap around and embrace and support one another like the cells in the nautilus, like the egg sac, like the lines in the carved horse's mane. Moore also responds to a very famous nineteenth-century poem by Oliver Wendell Holmes, "The Chambered Nautilus," with its inspirational ending: "Build thee more stately mansions, O my soul! . . . Till thou at length art free!" Holmes urges confidence and self-improvement, outgrowing one's outdated roles and shells, while Moore praises patient care for others. She is no enemy of classical beauty, but she wants to recuperate it for herself, and for her mother, or for all mothers, rather than reserving it for maidens or heroes or men. The lines, like the good mother here, like the mythical horse, do more than support their rider; even their flaws make them beautiful, part of the total impression that her involuted, wraparound sentences give.

Constraint prompts invention; invention can spur delight. Forms that revel in their closure, forms that let poets show us they've done something difficult, drive poets to discoveries: that's just as true for Moore's elaborate syllabics as it is for Yeats's ottava rima or Charleston's "Spell Check." John Ashbery once compared writing sestinas to "riding downhill on a bicycle and having the pedals push your feet. I wanted my feet to be pushed." But form and closure, like bicycle pedals, can also get in the way. If you go to poetry seeking a vision of total freedom or of ceaseless defiance, in art or in life, you will likely be hostile to the kinds of form and the kinds of pleasure that I have been recommending throughout this chapter, no matter the poets' political views. And you might agree with the Mexican radical thinker and poet ~~Heriberto Yépez~~ (who prefers to print his name with strikethroughs). According to Yépez's 2017 volume *Transnational Battle Field*,

> FORM is designed to prevent expression
> of vulgar popular explosive unwelcomed forces.
> FORM will always be on the side of the enemy.
> As poets, here we are, on the wrong side.
> Poets, look around, you are surrounded
> by FORM's defense forces.
> Forget about FORM
> :::::::USE BOMBS::::::

Yépez appears to be arguing for, or gesturing toward, permanent revolution against the repetition of patterns, the establishment and perpetuation of rational order, predictable language, closure of any sort.

Few of us want to read a poem that consists of nothing but falling bombs; those of us (not me) who have lived amid literal bombs, or who have experienced the dissolution of literal day-to-day order, usually end up as vocal defenders of safety somewhere, predictability in some measure, even "form." That does not mean they will take any form they can get. Nor do we have to choose clear forms, forms with preexisting names, or kinds of poetry that require (as Moore's and Hayes's, Youn's and Yeats's do) closure; we can try to do something more evasive, something less legible, something more open-ended, something else. We can choose, not legible technical accomplishment, but intentional difficulty, poems that simulate chaos or make it impossible for us to say exactly what they mean or how they hold together. We will see some of those poems—and some reasons to like them, to seek them out— in chapter 4.

chapter four

DIFFICULTY

C HAPTER 3 SHOWED HOW SOME POEMS CAN NOT ONLY move us but also delight or astonish us, once we see them as displays of technique and skill, and how we can share and find pleasure in their kinds of play, their uses of constraint, their solutions to technical problems. This chapter shows how and why poets present *us* with problems, why some poets choose to write poems that do not make consistent sense, no matter how hard we work to untangle them. It shows how opaque or resistant language can instruct and delight, and how some non- or anti-sense in poetry can help us spot nonsense, or hypocrisy, or lies, in the rest of the world, outside poems.

The technically dazzling poems in chapter 3—and the ways we saw to appreciate their forms—suggest comparisons to other displays of technique, other ways to regard skillful play as beauty, from Mozart's sonatas to Simone Biles's floor routines. The poems in this chapter, instead, might suggest challenging, hard-to-interpret styles of modern dance; dissonant styles of modern music, from twelve-tone composition to sheets-of-noise rock; nonrepresentational painting and sculpture; nonnarrative theater or performance art; and challenges to our bodily routines, from meditation to ultramarathons. At times these difficult poems can also feel like semisecret codes, whispers, ciphers tapped out through walls, invitations to exciting rituals that only an in-group can find. Sometimes they suggest the difficulty in certain philosophical inquiries or meditative practices, which cannot and should not seem easy to understand. At other times difficult poems are more like political protests, direct actions: demonstrations that block traffic or jam the governor's phone lines in order to say or show how conventional wisdom and existing systems and easy understandings support the status quo, and to say that things should not go on as they are. Such weird, challenging poems want to stand in the way; they raise objections; they refuse to fit in.

Difficulty, impenetrability, the ideas that poets address a clique or an elite and that some poems are impossible to figure out; all these notions may seem modern, or modernist—part of the twentieth century—but they go back further than that. I begin with the incomprehensible, the challenging, the recherché, in poems written more than two hundred years ago, and then move forward to reasons for and kinds of difficulty. We'll see poems that imitate instrumental music; poems that allow several kinds of interpretation, from the philosophical to the sexual; poems that feel like attacks on ordinary language; and poems that present themselves as slippery codes to be shared among friends. We will see poems whose difficulty stems from, or mimics, their use of more than one language, and poems whose difficulty is existential, emotional, rather than semantic: not so much hard to interpret as hard to take. And I'll end with a poet not normally considered avant-garde or ultradifficult, and a poem that sums up several of the reasons that difficulty can give some poems not only an irreplaceable energy but also a way to resist bad ideas and bad societies, hence a reason to exist.

.

T. S. Eliot announced portentously in 1921 that "poets in our civilization, as it exists at present, must be difficult," because modern life was confusing and difficult too. The idea that new poems should be harder to read than prose, that serious poems pose a challenge to most readers, may seem like it began in the twentieth century, with the writers called high modernists (Eliot, Ezra Pound, Virginia Woolf, Gertrude Stein) who really did distance themselves from prose sense in new ways. And yet some poems have seemed hard to read for a while. Eliot made his announcement in the course of his essay "The Metaphysical Poets," about Donne and the contemporaries of Donne. Lord Byron, among the most popular poets of the early nineteenth century, complained in 1818 that William Wordsworth had grown incomprehensible:

> Wordsworth, in a rather long "Excursion"
>   (I think the quarto holds five hundred pages),
> Has given a sample from the vasty version
>   Of his new system to perplex the sages;
> 'Tis poetry—at least by his assertion,

And may appear so when the dog-star rages—
And he who understands it would be able
To add a story to the Tower of Babel.

Most readers who try *The Excursion* do find it hard going; almost all think it's too long. The earlier, more influential Wordsworth—the one who liked daffodils—can be a challenge too. Wordsworth and Coleridge's *Lyrical Ballads* (1798) consisted mostly of poems about peasants and rural scenes; its plain language seemed groundbreaking—or disturbing—for its apparent simplicity, like a Chuck Berry single on a playlist full of Frank Sinatra and Nat King Cole. It might have seemed, even, literally revolutionary: Wordsworth's new ways of writing about peasants and other low-status people came out of his sympathies with the French Revolution, which he and his friends first supported, then came to oppose. Peasants and other rural people, Wordsworth decided, were better subjects for poetry than city folk; they were closer to nature, to the real facts of real life and "the real language spoken by men" (as he put it).

And yet when William Wordsworth wrote about his own inward nature, his own thoughts, he could get complicated indeed. He and his sister in 1798 took a long walking tour along the River Wye, which separates England from Wales. William and Dorothy stopped for the view a few miles north of the ruins of a monastery called Tintern Abbey. William therefore called his poem "Lines Composed a Few Miles Above Tintern Abbey, on Revisiting the Banks of the Wye During a Tour, July 13, 1798"; it has been known, somewhat misleadingly, as "Tintern Abbey" since. The poem begins clearly enough:

Five years have past; five summers, with the length
Of five long winters! and again I hear
These waters, rolling from their mountain-springs
With a soft inland murmur.—Once again
Do I behold these steep and lofty cliffs,
That on a wild secluded scene impress
Thoughts of more deep seclusion; and connect
The landscape with the quiet of the sky.

Then it gets weird. Five years ago (the poem continues), Wordsworth had hiked the same riverbank in a mood of severe apprehension, "more like a man / Flying from something that he dreads, than one / Who sought the thing he loved" (he had just come back from postrevolutionary France). In 1798, though, things were different; because he was older, because he walked with his wise sister, because he had some distance from so many things he could never control, William could see things more philosophically. He had

        learned
To look on nature, not as in the hour
Of thoughtless youth; but hearing oftentimes
The still sad music of humanity,
Nor harsh nor grating, though of ample power
To chasten and subdue.—And I have felt
A presence that disturbs me with the joy
Of elevated thoughts; a sense sublime
Of something far more deeply interfused,
Whose dwelling is the light of setting suns,
And the round ocean and the living air,

And the blue sky, and in the mind of man:
A motion and a spirit, that impels
All thinking things, all objects of all thought,
And rolls through all things. Therefore am I still
A lover of the meadows and the woods
And mountains; and of all that we behold
From this green earth; of all the mighty world
Of eye, and ear,—both what they half create,
And what perceive.

"Nature," it seems, will take care of him; but how? William Empson complained that the lines did not make grammatical sense. "It is not certain what is far more deeply interfused than what," he mused. "It is not certain whether the music of humanity is the same as the presence. . . . The something may possibly dwell only in the natural objects mentioned, ending at sky; the motion and the spirit are then not thought of at all as interfused into nature, like the something; they are things active in the mind of man. At the same time they are similar to the something; thus Wordsworth either feels them or feels a sense of them." The supple blank verse (unrhymed iambic pentameter; don't confuse "blank verse" with "free verse") let Wordsworth stretch out, speculate, and explore his own thoughts; the results gave Empson a good, if snarky, example for *Seven Types of Ambiguity*, about how poets get useful effects from lines whose full sense will always be hard to decide.

Other critics treat the poet more respectfully, but they still disagree on just what he meant, which may prove Empson's point. Some of those critics focus on the long-suppressed, now amply verified story of Wordsworth's French lover, Annette Vallon, and their child, both of whom stayed in France when he moved away. My favorite Wordsworth expert, the Yale scholar Geoffrey Hartman, thought that nature, in the lines above, was teaching Wordsworth how to calm down, showing him that you could have a religious experience without blotting out or escaping from daily life. But that's not why those lines are in this book. Nor are they here because "Tintern Abbey" remains, two hundred years on, one of the most widely and deeply influential single poems in the history of English, though that's true too.

Instead, they're here because it's so hard to decide what they mean, and because so many people who can't quite decide nonetheless find them inspiring or exciting or consoling. The tough parsing does not point to one right answer (as, say, crossword puzzles do); the range of potential answers, their overlap and their penumbras, are what you discover by reading the poem. That wide range gives the poem what many readers (myself among them) have considered its warmth and its power. Dorothy Wordsworth remembered "Tintern Abbey" that way too. Decades later, quite ill, she wrote a short poem called "Thoughts on My Sick-Bed" about her memory of their walk; she "felt a power unfelt before" as she remembered "the green Banks of the Wye, / Recalling thy prophetic words." The poem carries some sense of revelation and prophecy, of something in poetry that remains deeply personal, vastly important, worth passing on, deeply tied up with difficulty or wordlessness, and thus impossible to spell out.

And that sense, that kind of ineffable spiritual difficulty, is one of the things that we mean when we call a writer or an attitude Romantic, whether or not the writer lived (like Wordsworth and Byron) during the Romantic period (from the French Revolution in 1789 through, roughly, the 1830s). You can trace Romantic attitudes from both Wordsworths, through Ralph Waldo Emerson, Walt Whitman, Emily Dickinson, and Herman Melville, up to Hart Crane, who during the 1920s tried to write poetry that was just as challenging as T. S. Eliot's but much more optimistic, and way more gay. More than once during Crane's short life, an editor agreed to publish his poems if and only if Crane could explain them in a letter. One of those poems was "At Melville's Tomb," which begins:

> Often beneath the wave, wide from this ledge
> The dice of drowned men's bones he saw bequeath
> An embassy. Their numbers as he watched,
> Beat on the dusty shore and were obscured.
>
> And wrecks passed without sound of bells,
> The calyx of death's bounty giving back
> A scattered chapter, livid hieroglyph,
> The portent wound in corridors of shells.

Here nature itself works like a difficult poem, its complex symbols yielding shifting, spiritually empowering, hard-to-process meanings. Had Crane sought similar verbal effects decades later, he might have labeled them psychedelic. We can decode them, nevertheless, within limits. Men taken by the sea's destructive randomness are both a legacy ("bequeathed") and an embassy to the nonhuman world undersea; when they die and the sea exposes their skeletons, their bones are white like dice (the first-ever dice were carved from bones). Melville's Captain Ahab was, presumably, a man on that kind of mission. A calyx (the part of a flower underneath the petals, the seat of its fertility) may take the same helical shape as a dangerous whirlpool; that whirlpool may kill sailors (who die without funereal bells) or give us back their corpses. Crane's poem invites that kind of intense decoding; at the same time, it presents a set of sublime hieroglyphs whose full meanings nobody will ever know.

Crane composed poems while listening, over and over, to orchestra music on 78 rpm records; other poets imitate music directly, trying to bypass semantic expression, not to need it, as instrumentals do not need words. Fred Moten's poems can sometimes be heard in that way: this very learned poet's work offers roomfuls of references, but it can also seem to keep a healthy distance from description, narration, exposition, and explanation, moving toward a challenge in pure sound, almost as jazz innovators like Ornette Coleman and Alice Coltrane moved their own performances toward a musical abstraction and away from conventional melody. Moten's poetry can also feel as if it is trying to describe itself, to give us the words for the ways in which its sounds move:

> let it go till it comes back again. it should be something on the wall, something on the floor should call itself when they break it down to put it back up again. when it comes back again it should be gone till it's all gone again and ready to return.

Again, from the same 2014 collection, *The Feel Trio*:

we study partial folds in them alpine jukes, bent, bow-
tongued stick and move and mahangonnic rupture in
september, in alabama, throat sung to the kabaret's general steppe and fade. out here you breathe they breath, this
bridge is just, this bridge is just a pile of bones this load be
breathing, this alpine rasp in this dry bridge just be weaving.

The first prose poem, using only the most common
words, seems to describe its own progress, its syntactic shape
as its sounds move through the air. The second does almost
the same thing but also scrambles into its mix a set of references to musical compositions and musical forms, especially
Bertolt Brecht and Kurt Weill's "Alabama Song" (also called
"Moon of Alabama") from *The Rise and Fall of the City of
Mahagonny*. The musical references (especially the repeated
"bridge": both a thing armies march over and part of a song)
suggest that we hear the poem as a kind of musical movement, carrying its enthusiasms, its apprehensions, in its tonal
highs and lows. We have to stop looking for prose sense to
apprehend what it does.

Reading Moten can feel like hearing complex music:
reading Rosmarie Waldrop can feel more like learning tough
math. Waldrop moved to the United States from Germany
as an adult along with her husband, the poet Keith Waldrop;
together they run the influential small press Burning Deck.
As teachers at Brown University they have encouraged or
launched three generations of demanding, slippery, or recal-
citrant writers, exposing them not only to English-language
modernism but to the sometimes greater challenges of

French- and German-language modernists such as Edmond Jabès, whom Rosmarie has translated. Almost all her own poems (like Jabès's) use blocks of prose; in them each sentence makes sense on its own, but the leaps between one and the next can strain our faculty for comprehension. Waldrop writes in a prose piece called "Driven to Abstraction":

> We take language for granted, as we do sitting and weeping. Unfamiliar speech we take for inarticulate gurgling. Filtered through sandbags.
>
> A searchlight beam makes a statement.
>
> The order of the world is so foreign to our subjective interests that we cannot imagine what it is like, says William James. We have to break it. Into histories, art, sciences or just plain rubble. Then we feel at home.

Such unsettled language might help us imagine an unbroken world (William James can help; we will see him again). Waldrop has written about "the empty space I place at the center of each poem to allow penetration." These moments of incomprehension do for her prose what line breaks do for lineated poems: they show us, as readers, that we can pause and return, that we are involved in deciding what we will let the world and the words in it do.

This kind of poetry, asking or requiring us to stop short, to go back, to reevaluate the sense we think we might have made of it, thus encourages us to go back, reevaluate, and critique the way we thought we understood—or accepted—other language, from the Pledge of Allegiance to the labels on prescription drugs. Waldrop writes elsewhere in "Driven to Abstraction,"

> Whereas the concept of spatial measurement does not conflict with that of spatial order, the concept of succession (bombings?) clashes with the concept of duration (US presence?).
>
> Tanks enter the discussion, and the case for absolute time collapses.
>
> We speak our own language exclusively. It embodies the universal form of human thought and logic.
>
> I toss in my sleep. As do many women.

Here each sentence alters the way the next, or the previous, sentence percolates through an attentive reader's mind. Is there a "universal form of . . . logic" (rather than one inflected by gender, by bodies and history)? Will war, like logic, always be with us? "Succession" means that something follows, or should follow, something else; what is supposed to follow from aerial attacks, and what does it mean to say that war can succeed?

This particular kind of difficulty—juxtaposing incompatible sentences, writing what cannot be true, ironizing everything, trying to call into question all or any truths—can mobilize outrage or embody frustration. It can also tell people erased by a consensus, made uncomfortable by prevailing wisdom, excluded by breezy generalization and inappropriate advice ("Everything works out for the best," "Get a good night's sleep," "God bless America," "Everybody loves Ray-mond"), that we are not alone.

These kinds of active resistance to prose sense often work best in prose poems, whose blocks or paragraphs do not come with the built-in pauses and breaks of poetic lines but offer the counterpoint of continuity. And prose poems like Moten's and Waldrop's, along with much of the present-day avant-garde, have a shared modern ancestor, not in Eliot (who generally liked rules), nor in Crane (who did not want any sharp break with the past), but in Gertrude Stein, whose first important book of poetry, *Tender Buttons* (1914), composed wholly in blocks of prose, sounds mostly like this:

A BOX.

Out of kindness comes redness and out of rudeness comes rapid same question, out of an eye comes research, out of selection comes painful cattle. So then the order is that a white way of being round is something suggesting a pin and is it disappointing, it is not, it is so rudimentary to be analysed and see a fine substance strangely, it is so earnest to have a green point not to red but to point again.

What on earth is happening here? Stein's first readers had no clue (the book received a smattering of baffled reviews). She became famous during her lifetime not as a poet but as a salon-giver, a Paris-based mentor for more popular writers (such as Ernest Hemingway), a sponsor of modernist paint-ers (such as Pablo Picasso), and an author of tricky but not overtly difficult books of prose, especially *The Autobiography of*

Alice B. Toklas (1933). After Stein's death in 1946, and especially after the 1960s, Stein began to look to some living poets like a good model for existential difficulty, the kind that just resists attempts to say what it means.

Tender Buttons might be the best place to begin reading this kind of writing, and this side of Stein. If it isn't for you, it will sound like it's all of a piece. If you come to love it and stick with it, you will start to see differences among Stein's works, as well as within the three parts of *Tender Buttons*, "Objects," "Food," and "Rooms" (the first two have many short sections; "A Box" is one). You will also come to know at least four different ways to interpret the weirdness in Stein, ways you can then bring to the gaggle of contemporary projects—Waldrop's and Moten's among them—that evolve from, or respond to, what Stein began.

The first way sees her writing as a kind of verbal cubism. Stein does with words what Picasso does with paint, viewing the material world (and the people in it) counterintuitively, sideways, backward, from contradictory angles, as they had never been viewed before. Stein's first serious readers, during her lifetime, tended to see her this way, which would make "A Box" some sort of attempt to describe an actual box, perhaps a breadbox or hatbox. Perhaps it has a red lining and holds something white made of leather ("painful cattle"), perhaps a hatpin or poinsettia (green and red). The process of removing something from a box, of opening a gift (say) seems "rudimentary," simple or preliminary; we have to look closely at that action, and at the box itself, to dislocate our ordinary habits of naming and framing, to see it anew.

No one can prove that "A Box" does *not* describe the opening of a real box, but the interpretive moves required to claim that it does may not be to everyone's taste. Other Steinians look at her early background in psychology and see her as a poet who tried to reframe, not boxes or roses or cattle, but the process of framing itself, the expectations and categories in play within a human mind. Stein attended medical school in Baltimore, although she did not graduate. At Radcliffe College during the 1890s she worked alongside the philosopher and psychologist William James when James was conducting experiments in psychology, some of which used automatic writing. Stein may have shared, early on, James's interest in what we don't know that we know, in how the mind uses categories we do not quite articulate or recognize. What if we try to recognize or to suspend the habits with which our brains usually sort the world? What will remain familiar? What will seem strange? Will the resulting sentences have subtexts, or rhythms, or moods? Her hard-to-parse lines slow down or arrest the psychology of perception so that we can consider how we feel and how we think, not only what we feel and what we think, and ask what each feeling in turn might "point . . . to . . . again." Can these kinds of sentences help us notice (as James put it) "a feeling of *if*, a feeling of *but*, and a feeling of *by*"?

No wonder this kind of writing gets called not only cubist but also experimental; it works like a psychology experiment. Can you make sense of this? What about *this*? Are you sure you're not just imposing your own assumptions? And this way of reading might lead us, as Waldrop did, to reconsider the assumptions we make about events far from Stein's poems. Stein was no political radical, but during the 1970s and afterward, contemporary poets who were or wanted to be politically radical found in Stein's experiments a set of techniques that look amenable to leftist politics because they train us to question everything. Stein's poems show us how to say, and how to have fun saying, "What?" or "Wait, what is that word doing there?" or "That word does not mean what you think it means," and if you can say that about red boxes, maybe you can say it about capitalism too. These poets use Stein-like moves to deconstruct, to burrow under or take apart, the ways in which other, more predictable language—the language of candidates for elective office, of advertising, of journalism— works. Stein's way of being canny about who is speaking, her distrust of distinct characters and realistic situations, might seem especially useful if you think (as some poets on the political left still think) that individual people, rights, and duties, speaking subjects with single voices, are a toxic illusion, or a bad way to think about the collective good.

And yet you can read much of Stein, and much of *Tender Buttons*, including "A Box," as having consistent subjects, describing things that individual characters do—especially sex. A box that is red on the inside and holds something pin-like; something that can solicit a lover's kindness, or redness, or rudeness; something normally closed off or concealed; something you might want to touch again and again ("point again") once you find it: What sort of thing could that be? When would you touch it? And why would an early twentieth-century lesbian writer choose to write about such things in a flirtatious, elaborate code?

Such questions answer themselves. They do not fit all Stein's poems. John Ashbery's favorite, *Stanzas in Meditation*, pretty much has to be read abstractly and philosophically. Stein's book-length poem *Lifting Belly*, on the other hand, is clearly erotica:

Kiss my lips. She did.

Kiss my lips again she did.

Kiss my lips over and over and over again she did.

I have feathers.

Gentle fishes . . .

Lifting belly is so strange.

I came to speak about it.

Selected raisins well then grapes grapes are good.

Much of Stein's poetry is harder to read for sex than *Lifting Belly*, but not that much harder, once you know how. A little later in *Tender Buttons* (to take another example almost at random) comes "A Substance in a Cushion." This poem (much longer than "A Box") reads, in part: "Callous is something that hardening leaves behind what will be soft if there is a genuine interest in there being present as many girls as men. . . . A sight a whole sight and a little groan grinding makes a trimming such a sweet singing trimming and a red thing not a round thing but a white thing, a red thing and a white thing." It's like a sex manual sent back and forth through Google Translate a few times and then read aloud at a special kind of a party, one where (to quote Stein once more) "the public is invited to dance."

We have been looking so far at lines, sentences, and entire poems that make it hard for us to decide what they mean. That kind of decision, that kind of assurance that you know what something means, is sometimes called closure; its opposite might be openness, in which phrases or sentences leave you hanging, keep you unsure about what or how much they mean. Closure and its opposite are not just properties of lines or sentences; you can have closure in comic book panels, for example, if you know what happened in between them, and openness if you have to guess. You have closure in a whole poem if (as Yeats said he wanted his own poems to do) it clicks like a box when you close the lid at the end. Conversely, a poem feels open, or lacks strong closure, if the end does not feel like The End: if it gives you the feeling (good or bad) that the writer has left threads dangling, that you must decide how best to interpret its disorder.

Poems—like other works of art—come with different kinds of closure, too. Sonnets come with strong closure; so do strongly plotted narrative forms like the classic detective story, which ends when and only when you know whodunit. Classic Victorian nonsense poems, like Lewis Carroll's "Jabberwocky" or Edward Lear's "The Jumblies," demonstrate strong sonic closure in their rhyming stanzas, and strong closure in plots ("Jabberwocky" is a conventional coming-of-age tale), even when their key nouns mean nothing at all. These poems' forms and sounds give you what you expect, even when their sense or story does not.

Writers who want to disrupt what you expect, to open up your expectations, may view formal closure (the kind that rhyme or shaped plot can give) as the enemy, as something that locks you out rather than letting you in, or as the opposite of Stein's invitation to dance. For such writers, ultraopen, hard-to-process, hard-to-unravel (or, perhaps, already-unraveled) art—I quote the Bay Area poet Lyn Hejinian in her 1983 talk "The Rejection of Closure"—"invites participation, rejects the authority of the writer over the reader and thus, by analogy, the authority implicit in other (social, economic, cultural) hierarchies."

You can find that kind of shockingly open (or hard-to-process or forever-confusing) text in many periods; you can even find it in classical antiquity, if you look hard enough for it and disregard what the authors probably wanted. Latter-day readers can find it in ancient Greek fragments, whose authors did not intend them to end where they ended for us now, where surviving text breaks off midphrase or midthought. Modern poets sometimes imitated those fragments, slyly or directly (as in Ezra Pound's jokey three-word poem "Papyrus"). You can find many more such radically open texts, texts whose last lines make you say not so much "Oh!" or "That's it!" or "Thank you" as "What???" or "That's all?" if you look among more recent poems. Hejinian's own book-length poem *My Life* (first published in 1980) consists of many disconnected sentences, each one relevant in some way either to the places where Hejinian has lived or to her psyche at various points in her life. The volume repeats a number of phrases unpredictably throughout its forty chapters (one for each year of her life), among them "As for we who love to be astonished" and "I wrote my name in every one of his books." Many sentences on their own feel like sweet childhood memories or perfectly comprehensible pieces of young adult angst. And yet the patterns that seem to hold the work together do not let us predict where it might end, nor do they help us guess what kind of sentence, what kind of content, will come next. Hejinian's *My Life* and its sequels (there is one, constructed on the same principles, entitled *My Life in the Nineties*) remain fun to read and reread, at least for me, for that play of clarity and unpredictability, that balance between not knowing how to take the work as a whole and recognizing—even seeing myself in—its separable, recombinant, open parts.

·

The authoritative literary critic George Steiner distinguished four kinds of literary difficulty. The first is contingent, like crosswords: a puzzle has a solution you can look up, a word has a rare meaning but you can find it, a cultural reference might be accessible to me but not to you. Not all such difficulties, not all such references, are matters of high culture, historic elites, educational privilege. "It's all on your apron, fool, the continent ejaculations, / the gizzard deportations, *el buche*, say it, *el buche*, / your gizzard neck—boy, that way I call the knowledge": so ends a sonnet by Juan Felipe Herrera called "Chicken Blood Townships," almost certainly about undocumented restaurant workers, in ways that you may or may not automatically recognize.

The second kind of difficulty is what Steiner calls modal, where we know what a sentence means literally but we don't know how to take it; is it a joke, a trial balloon, an experiment, a piece of sarcasm? The third is what Steiner calls tactical difficulty, the result of a writer trying to innovate, or to speak to an in-group: Gertrude Stein's strangeness might make a good example, whether you see it as cubist or as erotic or as both and more. Some poets even set out to create a style that's difficult, even incomprehensible, for a very large set of potential readers in order to speak to, or make sense for, or express solidarity with, a smaller set; such poets' contingent difficulties may show how, and why, some people's inward selves, deepest truths, and day-to-day experiences strike others as impossible to understand. Certain transgender poets, such as kari edwards and Cody-Rose Clevidence, come very close to defining transgender poetry in this way, as something that cisgender people perhaps can never understand: the inner truths of trans and nonbinary people (so these poets suggest) are truly new and strange and specialized, akin to science fiction, with concepts that come from another reality, or from the future: Clevidence hopes to create a "lucent cyborg . . . lonely in hologram," a "heartthrob in the cellular matrix . . . chemosocial to the core." (Other trans poets, such as Ari Banias and Joy Ladin, value accessibility and lucidity; trans poets today have several avenues for visibility and legibility, though we remember when we had none.)

Steiner's fourth type of difficulty is what he labels ontological: the difficulty we have in making sense of an ontologically difficult poem reflects the difficulty the poet herself has had in making sense of an unjust, incomprehensible, obdurate world. "Ontological difficulties," Steiner writes, "confront us with blank questions about the nature of human speech, about the status of significance, about the necessity and purpose of the construct which we have . . . come to perceive as a poem." Steiner's example is the almost undecodable language in the late poetry of Paul Celan, whose compound words, nonwords, and fractured stanzas can reflect his difficult life as a Holocaust survivor and as a Romanian Jewish poet writing in German. "In each poem," Celan himself remarked, "reality is checkmated once and for all." Celan is in nearly all ways an extreme; Steiner's categories are in part a power play, a way to suggest that other kinds of difficulty (like Stein's or edwards's) are less important than Celan's dense, grim, perhaps uninterpretable oeuvre. And yet the categories make sense, not so much as kinds of poems (like food groups: fruit, vegetables, grains, meat) but as qualities that you can find in poems (like vitamins: A, B_{12}, C, and so on).

You can find all four qualities all over the work of the contemporary West Coast poet Rae Armantrout, who makes obscure references; writes phrases that might or might not come from the same speaker, might or might not be sarcastic; emerged from an in-group devoted to Stein's legacies, radical politics, and other versions of late modernism; and reflects the ineradicable difficulty we may have in understanding one another, or our society, or the physical world. Armantrout's short poems often imagine a futile, or unending, or imperfect, resistance to very imperfect models, to bad understandings we already have. A recent poem called "Old School" reads, in part:

Pull strings taut and
something like
points reappear
in the model . . .

To aspirate
is to breathe in
and choke. Nobody
wants this.

The first stanza refers to physicists' superstring theory, which holds that besides three familiar dimensions of space (up and down, back and front, side to side) there are extra ones, coiled submicroscopically like tight balls of string. The same stanza's challenge to "the model" might be modal or tactical: Do you know anybody (say, a high school student) who seems stretched too thin or pulled taut by somebody else's aspirations, by a system and its model of success? Do you know anyone whose aspirations (whose hopes to rise in society or a profession) might be choking off the rest of their life? "Nobody wants this," such a person might say. But Armantrout does not just object to a particular institution (like a school or a profession). She also registers a clipped protest, complete with rough, raw, repeatedly jarring line breaks ("like / points"), against an entire "model" for how to live. What will become of such objections? Will things change? Armantrout concludes with another pun on physicists' terms (such as "conservation of energy"): "Nobody's listening // is conserved."

Steiner's four categories may sound as arbitrary as Empson's seven types of ambiguity: there could easily be six, or fifteen. The larger, almost inarguable point is that there are kinds of attractive difficulty, that each kind can bring some readers to some poems (while repelling others), and that if we can disaggregate some of the kinds, we will become able to talk about more poems, and about why some readers like or love them. Another kind of difficulty might be called expressive or even aggressive: the poem is difficult not in the sense of a difficult math problem (which you can solve) or a difficult problem in philosophy (which may not have a solution), nor in the sense of music that is hard to play, but in the sense of a difficult personality, a companion or friend or colleague or enemy who is or wants to be hard to take.

This is the kind of difficulty that has a kinship with skronky jazz, and avant-garde noise, and some hip-hop, and lots of punk rock. You can find a little of it in Moten and more of it in John Yau, whose poem "Ravings from a *Blacke Calender*" is an eleven-segment poem composed mostly of the one-line stanzas that critics call monostichs. Here are the first few segments:

1.
Better to put a safety pin through your lips than a nail
    in your right eye.

2.
Better to stamp on your ancestor's grave than be stopped
    in your neighbor's yard.

3.
I made a glyph for the brain when it's on fire.

4.

I copy down the sounds I hear inside my head,
the perfect copy I carry under my arm
when I want people to stay away.

The start of the fourth segment sounds almost naïve. But Yau
then turns the sentiment on its head, suggesting that the illeg-
ibility, the unapproachability, of the copy he makes is part of
the point. Nobody gets all the way inside that head; nobody
should—it's on fire.

Aggressive difficulty of this kind can become aggression
against the whole world, a kind of radical blowtorch or ba-
zooka against all of social life and language. Armantrout and
Hejinian emerged in the late 1970s from a set of controversial
writers sometimes called the language poets, after the mag-
azine *L=A=N=G=U=A=G=E*, published out of New York
by two other poets, Charles Bernstein and Bruce Andrews.
The language poets no longer seem as similar as they once
did, and the works of a few (especially Armantrout) seem
beautifully similar to the most challenging poems of centuries
past (Armantrout often, and rightly, gets likened to Dickinson). But all of the language writers shared a commitment to
modernist weirdness and progressive or radical politics, and
all paid attention to Gertrude Stein. Most of them wanted to
use their difficult language to push back against the obedience
to authority and the unconsidered, emotionally charged language ("defending democracy," for example) that sent Americans to die in Vietnam. And some of these writers maintained
aggression or sarcasm as the main note in their later work, as

in Andrews's book-length prose poem *I Don't Have Any Paper So Shut Up; or, Social Romanticism* (1992), where he writes (I take excerpts almost at random) "shake 'em on down thermidor eggs made from mud masturbate with a patent," "nameless hairless turkey—oil truck relieves a widow, evisceration was too good for him."

Difficult, cranky, over-the-top, chaotic poetry need not always sound like such an angry dude. The twenty-first-century poets whom Arielle Greenberg and Lara Glenum collect in their anthology *Gurlesque* use shock, confusion, and chaos for more playful and overtly feminists goals: they hope to liberate women and girls from the expectations of history, of coherence, of responsibility, imposed by patriarchy, or by history, or by men. As Greenberg and Glenum state in their introduction: "The Gurlesque was born of black organza witch costumes and the silver worn-out sequins mashed between scratchy pink tutu netting and velvet unicorn paintings and arena rock ballads and rainbow iron-on glitter decals and self-mutilation. . . . No means no, asshole. And yes means yes." The Gurlesque predates—but includes or resembles—a great deal of writing available now online, by poets who have not yet published a book. The category, at its broadest, includes poets we have already seen, such as Hera Lindsay Bird and Brenda Shaughnessy, as well as more disorienting, exhilarating, envelope-shredding poets such as Chelsey Minnis: "Sometimes I have to throw up and pass out in order to get to the next set of time increments. Because otherwise time forms into a hard migraine like a gumball, / I want to wear fluted sleeves and become like a darling person with appropriateness all around me . . . It is rough to be a seafoam wench."

That's an out-there, over-the-top, WTF attitude; it's also a version of feeling, a portrayal of exasperated desire—in other words, a poem that can be admired for its challenges, or appreciated as lyric, as an effort to put into words a specific emotion. Difficult poetry can be lyric poetry too: the same modern poets can appeal to one crowd for their weirdness and their challenge to existing conventions and to another crowd for their lyric qualities and emotional depth.

That double appeal helps explain why John Ashbery— no one's idea of a populist, or a clear, poet—remained so famous for so long. During the 1970s Ashbery won almost all the prizes that an American poet can win. For a few decades after that he was among the most widely admired and the most often imitated of American poets, although—or because—novices found his sentences hard to follow, their prose meanings—who did what to whom and where and why?—impossible to pin down. Reading a typical Ashbery poem means diving into a set of shifting pronouns, dangling deictics, and ambiguous allusions that could feel either confining or liberating, like a maze, or the back of a moving car, or an unsettling but pleasant dream. In the title poem from *As We Know* (1979),

All that we see is penetrated by it—
The distant treetops with their steeple (so
Innocent), the stair, the windows' fixed flashing—
Pierced full of holes by the evil that is not evil,
The romance that is not mysterious, the life that is not life,
A present that is elsewhere.

We never learn what "it" could mean. Ashbery's syntactic evasions mime the evasiveness of our own goals, the sliding imprecision of our own thoughts: What does it mean to feel that your life is not your life, that you are really already elsewhere? You can read these evasions as ways to represent those thoughts, or as a search for visionary symbols (like Crane's), or as a kind of low-key, continuous flirting, a way to make connections without committing the poet or reader to anything except the continued pleasure of mutual attention, of delightedly unfixed, forever-open response. As Ashbery puts it in "Train Rising Out of the Sea," his evasiveness "has a certain function, though an abstract one / Built to prevent you from being towed to shore." The same poem hopes, coyly, that "we may be friends."

Poets like Minnis, and Andrews, and Yau, and Ashbery can be read either expressively (they are showing you what it is like to be them, and it is difficult to be them; they are difficult, chaotic, extravagant, or often angry) or impersonally, as creators of projects designed to examine shared language, shared worlds. Rodrigo Toscano's *Explosion Rocks Springfield* insists that we see its challenge as the latter, looking not at its author, nor at our feelings, but at the kinds of events it (very obliquely) describes. The book contains sixty-six poems, or texts, each with the same title: "The Friday Evening Gas Explosion in Springfield Leveled a Strip Club Next to a Day Care." Some of these texts provoke questions about what we value in government and society; about zoning; about work and labor, paid and unpaid (Toscano is also a labor activist); about collective responsibility; about law and law enforcement; about who owns what and who lives where: "What did gas do to a pair of brownstones in the Brooklyn Township of Greenpoint that same night?" Other texts are . . . odder:

Why doink in croinky foinkiness?

Priday, the dearth after Pirsday, the fray before Paturday, always.

How goes PSHSHSHSHSHSHSHSH *in* there?

Escapes

In random patterns—for?

You *can* make phrase-by-phrase meaning out of this kind of writing, if you try very hard, but that kind of making might miss the point. As with Minnis, Toscano's stranded sentences constitute an outcry, a way to fight back against the ridiculousness of entrenched power, a kind of near-the-gallows humor, a joke passed around a protest (Toscano took part in Occupy Wall Street). It's hard for me to enjoy a lot of this kind of poetry at once—a bit goes a long way, and then I just want to read Keats—but I am glad to know it's out there.

Toscano looking at zoning, Stein at boxes, Crane at the sea: each of these poets, as far apart as they are in other respects, wants to use difficulty to help us reexamine, slowly or painfully, what we already think we see, so that we can notice either the injustice or the beauty that we would otherwise overlook. The goal of making the world weird again, either to like it more or to help it change, goes back at least a century: Russian modernists called it *ostranenie*, "making strange," and Wallace Stevens imagined that kind of work—the work of difficult modern poetry—as the work of an angel: "I am the necessary angel of Earth," says a spirit in one of Stevens's poems, "Since, in my sight, you see the Earth again."

Poets can bring that kind of slowed-down attention, that kind of refocused weirdness, not just to things of beauty or parts of society but to the materials that make up a poem: to ink and paper, to letters and parts of letters, to words as physical marks. e. e. cummings (who preferred to spell his name all lowercase) became famous during the twentieth century partly for writing charming poems of erotic desire, partly for de-forming syntax ("he sang his didn't he danced his did"), and partly for making aspects of poetry that had been the province of printers and publishers take on meaning within his poems. One of his best-known poems rearranges the letters in "grasshopper" in order to suggest a scrambled, excited, hopping motion: the poem begins "r-p-o-p-h-e-s-s-a-g-r" and continues, excitedly, "rea(be)rran(com)gi(e)ngly," through fourteen more lines.

Other poets use the resources of print, layout, and typography in ways that pose deeper challenges. Craig Santos Perez first got noticed for long poems full of facts about the troubled history of Guåhan (Guam), where he grew up. Perez, who now teaches at the University of Hawai'i, has not abandoned any of those concerns, but he has sharpened his tools and expanded his range. You have to slow down a great deal, to attend to the physical page, to read English as if it were a language you had not yet fully acquired, in order to process all the two-character slices of this recent poem, which also incorporates terms from the island's ancestral language, Chamoru:

(i tinituhon)

~

fu	ll	br	ea	th	in	gm	oo
nw	he	re	do	is	la	nd	sb
eg	in	sp	ir	al	ti	me	wa
ve	co	nt	ra	ct	io	ns	ar
ri	va	l3	0m	in	ut	es	ap
ar	t"	ha	ch	a"	th	ea	lp
ha	be	t,	ac	on	st	el	la
ti	on	of	bo	ne	ho	ok	so
ri	gi	ŋ"	hu	ng	ga	n"	so
un	dm	ea	su	re	sa	mn	io
ti	cf	lu	id	is	90	%w	at
er	sh	ou	ld	[w	e]	go	to
th	eh	os	pi	ta	l		

The difficult process of turning paired marks into words ends up suggesting at once the difficult process of learning to read a new language, the psychologically difficult process of realizing that you are going to become a parent, and the physically difficult process of exhaling and inhaling when you, yourself, are pregnant and ready to give birth. The place of "islands" in the Pacific Ocean, in the collection of oceans that spans the globe, suggests the place of a fetus in the salty "amniotic fluid" of the womb, where no one or everyone has been an island; the single Chamoru words are like islands, like Guåhan itself in a sea of imperial English. "I tinituhon" means "the beginning"; "hacha" is the numeral one, and "hunggan" one of several Chamoru words that mean "yes." And the bizarre typography, the grid of doubled letters (like paired parents) whose patterns do not match up with the patterns of words, suggests how tough many of us (especially those without much social privilege) find it to make the patterns we want in our lives, or in the lives of our children, match up with the patterns we get.

Perez has written a poem that's hard to read, about experiences that must have been not just cognitively but emotionally hard: becoming a parent and watching your partner give birth. Such poems challenge us when we try to talk about them, not because their prose meanings are hard to decode but because they reveal, or investigate, parts of the poet, or of ourselves, or of our culture, that are hard to articulate, hard to admit. They are the kinds of poems, the kind of experiences, that Wordsworth meant when he ended a famous poem (not "Tintern Abbey") by invoking "thoughts that do often lie too deep for tears."

For the New Zealand poet James K. Baxter, those kinds of difficulties—not semantic but spiritual—lie at the heart of all genuine literature. "Poems come," he wrote in 1964, "out of the chaos inside people, which the ordered world around us has no use for. . . . One has to abandon all ready-made answers in order to go into the dark place where the poem begins." Having become by some measures his country's leading poet, despite (and by writing about) his alcoholism, his inner divisions, and his complicated family, Baxter in 1968 had a vision that told him to leave his old life, learn te reo Māori (the Māori language), and found a commune at a remote site beside a convent called Jerusalem, on the Whanganui River. He really did all these things, and wrote poems about doing them, copiously, until his death from exhaustion in 1972. These poems—still revered in New Zealand, not nearly famous enough in the rest of the world—combine in their (mostly) unrhymed sonnets and couplets the physical difficulties of hard rural life; the practical difficulties of sheltering, feeding, and caring for dozens of well-meaning hippies; the intellectual difficulty of knowing you write, and think, in the language of empire, in land that your ancestors (at least arguably) stole; and the emotional difficulty of Baxter's demanding, antinomian, left-wing Catholic faith.

One of the last Jerusalem poems, a sonnet sequence entitled "Te Whiore o te Kuri" ("The Tail of the Dog"), considers the bodily risks we can take (or refuse) for others and the psychological pain when we realize that our lives, and the lives of our friends, and ultimately our way of life, will not endure. Here is its fourth segment:

The rain falls all day. Now the tanks will be full.
The road down river will turn to wet porridge

And the slips begin. Herewini told me
How Te Atua warned him that the bank would fall,

So he left the grader and came to shift his mates,—
They ran to safety and the bank did fall

Silently, eighty tons of earth and boulders,
Burying him to the armpits. His leg is still blue

Where the great stone cracked it and the bolts were put
    through the bone,
But he can walk on it. The drips from the holes in the roof

Spatter in the kitchen, on the boards behind the stove,
At the foot of Francie's bed. Beyond the lid of cloud

I hear the droning of the birds of Armageddon,
That one day will end the world we understand.

Herewini and Francie are personal names, but Te Atua is not—it can mean the Christian God, or Jesus, or a powerful spirit of any sort, one who might love us or leave us to our fates. This unrhymed sonnet about them, and about Baxter's vocation, belongs with other difficult poems not because (as with Stein) it's hard to wrestle into much prose sense, but because its simple prose sense points so insistently to so many parts of life that are hard to accept, and even harder to deny. Does Baxter want to be like Herewini? Can he save his friends, or his commune, or civilization (whatever that means)? Can you? We all depend on what we cannot control, from the water level in cisterns or reservoirs to the passability of roads to the kindness of strangers, and someday one of these things will run out. We endanger ourselves if we take risks for others, with our strength, our trust, or our time, and we might not save them anyway; the poem is tough to interpret because when Armageddon—or for that matter authoritarian government—looms, it is tough to know what we should do. The raindrops and birdsong match the repeated hard consonants (the *t* in "tanks," "wet," "shift," "tons"; the *d* in "drips," "lid," "cloud," "droning," "Armageddon," "understand"); Baxter's closing hexameters drive the hardest points home.

We have seen many kinds of difficulty so far—the amicable, the inviting, the aggressive, the visionary, the sensual, the intoxicating, the recherché. All of them, though, might be said to have the same opposite, to react against the same kind of thing: the classical, transparent, easy-to-understand poem, the poem that invites us to take it all in at first reading, to admire its apparently perfect (as table manners are perfect) form, to assume that problems have solutions, and questions have answers, within the world that the poem invites us to see. Few American poets during the twentieth century understood that elegant, reasonable, transparent, classical, formal ideal better than the young Adrienne Rich. Rich's 1951 poem "At a Bach Concert" spells out, almost baldly, the doctrine that poetic style reflects a just society and an appropriate way of life, everything in its place:

> Form is the ultimate gift that love can offer,
> The vital union of necessity
> With all that we desire, all we suffer.
>
> A too-compassionate art is half an art.
> Only such proud restraining purity
> Restrains the else-betrayed, too human heart.

These lines say not just what Adrienne Rich then believed, or wanted to use her skill set to make herself believe, but what many students and young writers were taught in the universities (and schools and places of worship) of the 1950s, what many are still taught today. Art exists in order to offer a comprehensible, beautiful vision of order; tragedy is the highest and aptest of stories; the highest virtue is self-restraint; and if we do not fit the forms of already-existing poems or homes or schools or jobs, if other people cannot understand who we are, what we want, or who we want to be, our art should try to help us hide or change.

It's another Luke Skywalker moment: every word in that last sentence is wrong. So, at least, Rich later decided. Some of the poems that grew out of those decisions, and out of her mature commitment to feminism and queer liberation, pursue a fierce clarity designed to show other people how her struggle felt. Other poems, though, work hard to depict her own internal divisions, and to overturn or demolish—they really had harmed her—traditional, inherited, supposedly stable or fixed ways to live and to write. You can watch her summon that kind of trouble in the 1970 poem she called, after Donne, "A Valediction Forbidding Mourning":

My swirling wants. Your frozen lips.
The grammar turned and attacked me.
Themes, written under duress.
Emptiness of the notations.

They gave me a drug that slowed the healing of wounds.

I want you to see this before I leave:
the experience of repetition as death
the failure of criticism to locate the pain
the poster in the bus that said:
my bleeding is under control.

A red plant in a cemetery of plastic wreaths.

A last attempt: the language is a dialect called metaphor.
These images go unglossed: hair, glacier, flashlight.
When I think of a landscape I am thinking of a time.
When I talk of taking a trip I mean forever.
I could say: those mountains have a meaning
but further than that I could not say.

To do something very common, in my own way.

Everything about the poem suggests rejection, from its spondaic opening to its forceful, irregularly paced, isolated lines. Rich rejects the traditions—of formal intricacy, of poetic closure, of cisheteronormative love and marriage and history and fidelity, of complexity that will always make *sense*—that Donne, for a writer of Rich's generation (whose mentors saw Donne as a model), could represent. A valediction, as in Donne, is a goodbye, and Rich is saying goodbye at once to a lover—she will not go back—and to the ways of writing that marked her previous, more conventional life.

For the Rich of this poem—who had not yet come out as lesbian—many forces and structures and parts of society had worked in sync to keep her, and people like her (women, wives, mothers, women writers), down. Liberation from all those structures would therefore require—and might sound like—disharmony, chaos, a series of salvos and semantic bursts that do not cohere as Donne's poems, or Rich's early poems, cohered. It's a wreck, but a wreck with a direction, "away": away from the "themes written under duress," where "themes" means both "morals" and "college essays" (Yale still has a writing course called Daily Themes); away from the empty notations of literary love; away from the prescriptions of male obstetricians and gynecologists; from well-meaning husbands and friends; from what Rich would name in a 1980 essay "compulsory heterosexuality"; from the insistence that already-existing ways of reading, and already-existing ways of life (the ones she, and I, were raised to understand), are all there is, and always have been.

These ways of life hurt us and then sell us healing balm; they break us apart and then try to sell us the glue. You can read Rich's valediction as expressive, as aggressive, like Yau's, or as a challenge to cognitive habits, like Waldrop's; as a form of covert alliance, like Ashbery's, or as an invitation to set off on your own, to leave the society and tradition that produced Donne and Christmas and isolated nuclear families and un-equal marriages and homophobia and the feminine mystique. This kind of departure is "something very common"—people quit, or walk out, or break up, all the time—but it's also unique, "in my own way." And it has to be accomplished aggressively, in pieces, as a series of hard-to-put-together fragments, as a difficult departure from consecutive, cohesive sense.

There's some irony in how Rich makes Donne not only her source but her target, since Donne himself (as we saw in chapter 1) could also represent resistance to received ideas, along with sexual or religious liberation. But that's not what Donne seems to mean for Rich; it's not the context that his poetry had for her. And all literary traditions, all poems, come to us in some context, within some situation—in this book, on a test, in an anthology, in a beat-up paperback, on some-one's Instagram. Critics can try to extricate poems from in-appropriate, unflattering situations, from ways in which those poets have been misunderstood, but we may not always be able to do that job; sometimes we should not.

That's because the reading of poetry, like the reading of anything, takes place in history; we are who we are before we come to the poem, and we belong, or want to belong, to communities that exist when we are not reading. That's why, again, a poem that sounds difficult to one reader—because it deploys unfamiliar techniques or sounds "wrong" across centuries or oceans, or because it contains Spanish or te reo Māori or scientific terms—might sound easy or natural to another. It's a truth to keep in mind when enjoying, or rec-ommending, or complaining about, many difficult poems. As we've seen, the facts of exclusion and inclusion, the way that some forms of language can invite us in or keep us out, pro-vide the *subjects* for some of our strangest poems.

Another truth—equally there in Yau and in Stein and in Wordsworth—is that difficulty, whether aggressive or inviting, whether expressively rich or deliberately ascetic, works best when we see what it works *against*: what the poet wants to resist, or escape, or avoid, or take down, or dissolve, or start a revolution to overcome. Almost all the poems we have seen in this chapter work as attacks or counterattacks, as mysteries without solutions, as evocations of the indescribable, or as ways to raise questions, to ask us to look again. What hap-pens, though, after we have looked again at the complex map of social possibilities, and we want poems to help us decide where to go? What happens when we ask poems not for new questions but for usable answers, when we want poems that offer us guidance or help us decide (to quote another title of Wallace Stevens's) "How to Live. What to Do"? We can find those answers in old poems and in new ones; we will see some of those poems in chapter 5.

chapter five

WISDOM

D O POEMS HAVE MESSAGES? DO THE MESSAGES MATTER?
When should we ask poems to guide, not our feelings alone or our memories, but our beliefs and our
behavior—to tell us, in general terms, what we can or should
do? "If you want to send a message," the saying goes, "call
Western Union." But Western Union sent its last telegram in
2006; people still write poems, and some embody messages.
They ask us to act in a certain way, to serve God or treat children gently or start revolutions or reconcile ourselves to the
weak creatures that we are. Some teachers tell students that all
poems and stories have messages; others insist that none do.
I disagree; various poems work in various ways, toward various goals, despite their shared technical repertoire and their
shared literary history.

Some poems contain quotable messages; others do not.
You might share some poems with friends not, or not only,

because you find them intricately beautiful, not or not only because you see yourself or encounter a friend in them, but because they help you take risks, handle grief, keep a friend, change society, or sort out your complicated life. For every writer who claims, as John Keats did, to "hate poetry that has a palpable design upon us," there is another who, like Allen Ginsberg in "Sunflower Sutra," hopes to deliver "my sermon to my soul." This chapter will look at the poems that fall closer to Ginsberg, at how poems can frame, contain, and imply directions for life: in other words, wisdom—claims about how to act and what to believe.

I'll start with the short forms of poetic wisdom that come to us from antiquity and then look at how some contemporary poets frame general advice. I'll look at the way that some advice—and forms designed to convey that advice—get reused, quoted, and undercut within poems we can enjoy for their attitudes, even for their snark. I'll look at a popular Victorian poet to see how he gave such effective, wise advice (so his contemporaneous readers believed). Finally, I'll look at a contemporary poet to see how the usable wisdom she offers gets woven in with idiosyncratic expression and with calls for timely political action.

•

If you want a compact, aurally intricate representation of somebody's interior life, poems might well be the first place you look. The same holds if you're looking for perfectly executed terza rima or for a bracing challenge to all storytelling, to all prose sense. But if you want wisdom, words about how to live, you can go to your friends, or to novels, or to memoirs, or to sermons, or even, these days, to quality TV. Why seek it—why, if you write, embed it—in poems?

One answer is memorability: poetic techniques make language easier to remember or take to heart. Oral cultures (cultures without writing) require this feature, since, by definition, they preserve only the language that people remember. In cultures with writing systems, the same aspects that make verse memorable when heard make it more likely to be recorded and reread. "Of two descriptions, either of passions, manners, or characters, each of them equally well executed, the one in prose and the other in verse, the verse will be read a hundred times where the prose is read once." That's William Wordsworth, in the 1800 preface to *Lyrical Ballads*. Wordsworth also believed—and he may have been right—that hard truths, painful subjects, and tough-to-swallow claims could be easier to handle, less likely to make you turn away, when handled in verse, since the formal properties of verse mix pleasure with anything, even "the deeper passions" and their pains.

Things said in poems also get changed by their place in poems, ironized, qualified, undermined, reinforced, or made other than literal, not by the mere fact that they show up there but by the other statements, symbols, characters, and sound effects around them. We've already seen how poems can feel like—or become—magic spells; that property also means they can seem to do, or feel like they do, what older cultures have tried to use magic to do: poems can execute curses or blessings, ceremonies or prayers. Even without those effects, the formal language in many poems can fit formal occasions—they can seem right (so to speak) for weddings and a funeral, as well as for ceremonies of other kinds.

This book started with lyric poetry, apparently personal and clearly emotional; this chapter starts with sayings, proverbs, and apparently impersonal wisdom. These functions for verse, and for memorable language (even if it gets inscribed as prose), carry over into the oldest surviving written texts, into Sumerian hymns and sayings, for example: "In a city with no dogs, the fox is boss" (translated by Jon Taylor). Those kinds of evocative, figurative declarations often come in long collections of very short forms preserved since antiquity, as in the biblical books called (in English) Proverbs and Ecclesiastes, or in the Daodejing (Tao-te Ching). They may try to change our behavior, or hold us to rules, or acknowledge our ordained fate, as in this early Islamic quatrain translated by Abdelfattah Kilito and Robyn Creswell:

> We are the children of the earth and its residents.
> We were created of earth and to earth we shall return.
> Good fortune never lasts long for humankind,
> And bad fortune is undone by nights of happiness.

This poet, known as al-Ma'arri, does not so much show you who you are (as in the poems we saw in chapters 1 and 2) as write to help you live with it; he aims to help you, to help any of us, calm down, step back, and live with sometimes-bitter truth.

Such wisdom has direct parallels from many cultures and many kinds of poems, sacred and secular, among them Jewish liturgy and the Anglo-Saxon poem entitled "Deor," whose refrain says (translated into modern English), "That changed; this may, too" ("Þæs ofereode, / þisses swa mæg"). Once poets' advice, words of wisdom, gets established as its own genres (epigrams, apothegms, verse proverbs), later poets can alter or respond. In the biblical book of Ecclesiastes, prudential counsel (calm down; this life's not easy) and potentially pious advice (care less for this world and, perhaps, more for another) keeps slipping or sliding into something more like despair:

> All the rivers run into the sea; yet the sea is not full;
> unto the place from whence the rivers come, thither they
> return again.
> All things are full of labour; man cannot utter it: the
> eye is not satisfied with seeing, nor the ear filled with
> hearing.
> The thing that hath been, it is that which shall be; and
> that which is done is that which shall be done: and there is
> no new thing under the sun.

These lines or sentences from the King James Version of Ecclesiastes 1:7–9 may be printed as verse or prose. They also turn up in a handful of pop songs (Jay Livingston and Ray Evans's "Que Será Será"; Angel Olsen's "Heart Shaped Face"; "The Sea Refuses No River," by Pete Townshend of the Who). Writings like these from the ancient Near East also give models for later collections of sayings, some of them clear and other deeply ambiguous, as in William Blake's "Auguries of Innocence":

> A Robin Red breast in a Cage
> Puts all Heaven in a Rage. . . .
> The Bat that flits at close of Eve
> Has left the Brain that wont Believe.

You can find in these short units models for feeling. You can admire their parallel elegance. But they would not exist were it not for the wisdom they also try to convey. Later poets can, as Blake did, model their own works on these sayings, making them additionally memorable with single images, single rhymes. The disparate creators of modern African poetry in English often drew on forms and stores of proverbs less familiar to most US readers. Okot p'Bitek's *Song of Lawino* (1966), for example, is constantly quoting Acholi sayings: "Who has discovered the medicine for thirst?" Modern poets can also arrange to undercut traditional sayings by placing them in the mouths of untrustworthy characters, as when Robert Frost has a character in his often-misunderstood poem "Mending Wall" repeat "Good fences make good neighbors." And they can repurpose sayings, pieces of supposed wisdom, by arranging them into patterns that their sources could not have imagined or approved. The Singaporean poet Ng Yi-Sheng opens one poem about lost love, "Vacation," with a straightforward quip, reminiscent of Okot's: "There is no travel insurance for heartbreak." But he assembles another poem entirely out of single-line quotations from Singapore's long-serving prime minister, Lee Kuan Yew, under whose regime homosexuality remained illegal:

If nobody is afraid of me, I'm meaningless. . . .
No, it's not a lifestyle.
I neither deny nor accept that there is a God.
I will make him crawl on his bended knees, and beg
    for mercy.

The poet entitles this ironic assemblage "Like Making Love, It Is Always Easier the Second Time."

There are many ways to put wisdom into self-sufficient short forms. Gary Saul Morson, a scholar of Russian literature, has even compiled a taxonomy of them in verse and prose—the aphorism, the witticism, the apothegm, the proverb, each set apart from the rest by such features as whether it seems novel or traditional, double-edged or unambiguous, practical or otherworldly. Some wisdom traditions come with their own verse forms; how the lines sound depends on what language they use. Wisdom verse, like all verse in biblical Hebrew, often involves two-part lines. In modern and Middle English, we tend to get rhyme. Langston Hughes gave general advice, or practical counsel, for the readers he identifies as "we" (maybe everyone; maybe just African Americans) through a lattice of rhyme over one extended metaphor:

Freedom
Is just frosting
On somebody else's
Cake—
And so must be
Till we
Learn how to
Bake.

As in much of his work, Hughes's "we" applies to African Americans in his own era, but it need not apply only to them. The first part of this poem, called "Frosting," seems to disparage "freedom"; the second redefines it as something substantial that you—or "we"—have to create, using our own recipes. It sounds like work. But the result is sweet.

You can build a whole poem—as Hughes did—around one piece of advice, one sentence, one metaphor. You can also compile a poem by stacking or stringing together quotable units of wisdom, like Legos, with the expectation that some readers will enjoy the poem (or the Lego creation) as a whole and others will take it apart in order to use the bricks in their own creations. Eighteenth-century poets composed a lot of poems that way. Thomas Gray's "Elegy in a Country Church-yard" (1750), with its solidly detachable quatrains, became one of the most popular poems of his era in part because so many of its units lend themselves to quotation; they might fit into a sermon or into a letter from a parent to an adult child. Gray's poet mourns a dead peasant who never had the chance to get rich, or famous, or artistically prominent, because he grew up too far from learning and privilege:

> The boast of heraldry, the pomp of pow'r,
> And all that beauty, all that wealth e'er gave,
> Awaits alike th' inevitable hour.
> The paths of glory lead but to the grave....
>
> Full many a gem of purest ray serene,
> The dark unfathom'd caves of ocean bear:
> Full many a flow'r is born to blush unseen,
> And waste its sweetness on the desert air.

William Empson, in a glorious political rant from 1935, objected to these famous lines, then decided that they held wisdom after all: "By comparing the social arrangement [of eighteenth-century Britain] to Nature, [Gray] makes it seem inevitable, which it was not, and gives it a dignity which was undeserved. Furthermore, a gem does not mind being in a cave and a flower prefers not to be picked; we feel that the man is like the flower, as short-lived, natural and valuable, and this tricks us into feeling that he is better off without opportunities." And yet (Empson went on) Gray presented "one of the permanent truths; it is only in degree that any improvement of society could prevent wastage of human powers; the waste even in a fortunate life, the isolation even of a life rich in intimacy, cannot but be felt deeply, and is the central feeling of tragedy."

Evaluating, while describing, Gray's lines, Empson is really evaluating society. He hears the lines not as exercises, nor as versions of feeling or characters, but as directions for how to treat the communities in which we live. Are they static and unalterable, their failings simply tragic? Or are they unjust arrangements that we can change? Other poets of wisdom in short forms ask us to step outside our own first reaction, to contrast our feelings with other people's feelings, and then to let our own feelings go. Consider Mary Leader's "Bride, Wife, Widow":

I adore the way
He hums when he shaves, his
Deep voice, his small, lotioned hands.

I detest the way he hums when he shaves,
His deep voice, his small
Lotioned hands.

I miss the way he hummed
When he shaved, or did any
Small thing with his hands.

The three stanzas use almost all the same words, in almost the same order: the husband does not change until death changes him. What changes is the verb that follows "I." That last line break ("any / Small thing") carries the weight and the wisdom, and acts as an ingenious, pointed warning to those of us whose partners are healthy, or present, or alive. If something annoys you about your partner (it says), imagine how you might feel if that partner were gone.

Other modern poets of wisdom come across less as ingenious than as ingenuous. Poets who want you to celebrate their technique (like those we saw in chapter 3) run the risk of turning your attention away from whatever they want to say. Poems devoted to wisdom, poems that try to tell you something the poet believes you should know, may therefore lean in the opposite direction, looking or sounding artless, unpolished, raw. Almost every trend toward moral seriousness or wisdom, at least in English-language poetry, has looked at the time—if you weren't a fan—like a refusal to learn the rules: the young Wordsworth, the early William Carlos Williams, the Beats in the 1950s, slam and performance-oriented poets more recently, all were accused of not really counting as poetry, of blurting or stating whatever they wanted to say.

In fact these poets, at their best, were making up new rules, eschewing the quasi-professional authority of technique (the kind of authority we saw in chapter 3) for the moral authority that accrues, in our time, to outsiders. You can see these new rules in operation right now, in the work of young poets who grew up on stage and have now begun to publish books: in Danez Smith, for example, who concludes his sequence "Pitch for a Movie: Lion King in the Hood" with elegant and heartbreaking instructions:

> say the name
> of the first boy
> you love
> who died. . . .
> say it
> & love
> the air
> around your tongue.

New styles designed to give urgent assistance to readers may sound spontaneous, or messy, or unsubtle, compared to the old, even when they have little to do with performance out loud. Take the start of Paul Killebrew's poem "Noon Knowledge":

> When we felt like this
> This feeling that no
> It would never feel natural
> But what about possible
> To experience eyes open
> Somewhere close to acceptance

Real openness to experience, real understanding, will not feel slick or smooth or "natural"; it will feel awkward, and it will require, as Killebrew writes elsewhere, "a new form / Transparent deliberate amateurish." He does as another contemporary poet, Brenda Hillman, asks that we all do: "Write from where you are / Write what you want to read."

Contemporary poets—that is, *we*—are writing what we want to read, as Gray and Blake were more than two centuries ago. We are writing, as well, what we want to tell ourselves and what we believe that other people (not necessarily poets) need to know (Gray's elegy is sometimes read as a morality play about humility, sometimes as the poet's barely disguised meditation on his own demise). Such poems may assume many attitudes, from rough haste to apostolic gravity to an over-the-top sincerity, like the style Ross Gay adopts in *Catalog of Unabashed Gratitude* (2016):

> I am trying, I think, to forgive myself
> for something I don't know what.
> But what I do know is that I love the moment when
>   the poet says
> *I am trying to do this*
> or *I am trying to do that.*
> Sometimes it's a horseshit trick. But sometimes
> it's a way by which the poet says
> I wish I could tell you,
> truly, of the little factory
> in my head: the smokestacks
> chuffing, the dandelions
> and purslane and willows of sweet clover
> prying through the blacktop.

Notice how much work the word "horseshit" does in preventing the poem from turning saccharine; and of course horseshit can help the flowers grow. The garden (with help from horseshit) is, like the factory, making things other people might like or use.

Gay's kind of modern wisdom may be wholly secular, derived from this-worldly experience or from private intuition. But it may also feel like a sermon, or a revelation, or a prayer, or an appeal to a semidivine authority. The wisdom some poems convey can feel like religion, either because (as with George Herbert and Christina Rossetti and Donald Revell and so many others) the poets draw on their own religious beliefs, or because the poets' authority seems to stand in for the voice of revealed religion. Romantic and later nineteenth-century writers sometimes asked poetry to take the place of religion, binding us together, giving us purpose, providing ethical guidance, or lifting us above our practical cares: Matthew Arnold even predicted in 1880 that "most of what now passes with us for religion and philosophy will be replaced by poetry." Decades earlier, Arnold had written what remains, by far, his most famous poem, "Dover Beach," a yearning declaration of love in which he found time to bemoan the ebbing of "the Sea of Faith": love and poetry together, or perhaps love expressed through poetry, would let us "be true / To one another!" while the rest of the universe, and an absent God, let us down.

Arnold's hopes that poetry, as such, could make us better, more trustworthy, more spiritually complete, echo today through every contemporary teacher, TV presenter, and radio host who associates poems, or poets, or the word *poetry*, with moral authority and spiritual uplift. Taken in general terms, Arnold's predictions were a big mistake; their misplaced expectations created the kind of beliefs about "poetry," in general, that I have written this book in part to dispel. T. S. Eliot lit into those expectations with the energy of a writer who really needed (and, ultimately, found) explicit religious faith: "Nothing in this world or the next," he snapped at Arnold, "is a substitute for anything else." If you want spirituality or God, look for spirituality or God; do not assume that ethical advice, or general claims about human nature on this earth, or aesthetic experience (in songs, in dances, in graphic novels, in poems) will do the work that religion has done.

And yet individual poets—especially but not only during the nineteenth century—picked up a great deal of their appeal, then and now, by doing for some readers some of the things that religion can do for regular attendees at shul, at church, at the mosque, providing aesthetic experience, conveying beauty, but also organizing their lives and helping them decide how to be good, or just how to live. Henry Wadsworth Longfellow became the most popular poet of the American nineteenth century partly by providing these sorts of lessons, especially in his earlier poems. "Let us, then, be up and doing / With a heart for any fate!" exhorts the once wildly popular "A Psalm of Life" (1838). Another early poem, "Excelsior!"—Latin for "higher/better"—honors a mountain climber who died in the attempt, because he tried to better himself by something hard. Stan Lee almost certainly took the Marvel Comics slogan "Excelsior!" from Longfellow's poem. W. E. Henley's "Invictus" (1875) was once even more popular than those Longfellow poems; Henley's quatrains (concluding "I am the master of my fate, / I am the captain of my soul") have shown up in contexts as public and as various as speeches by Winston Churchill, Nelson Mandela, and Barack Obama; the Hollywood films *Casablanca* and *The Big Short*; the video game series *Mass Effect*; and the great early lesbian novel *Annie on My Mind*.

Such inspirational, quotable, popular verse became a target for twentieth-century critics who wanted their readers, and their students, to stop liking such easy-to-like poems, with their built-in sermons and clear advice. These critics wanted readers to admire, instead, the indirect or subtler triumphs of modernist poets like T. S. Eliot and Marianne Moore. And yet this didactic or homiletic strand in the making of English-language verse has never disappeared: you can find it in Moore herself, as well as in Ross Gay and in the very most popular poets of the 2010s, such as Mary Oliver and Rupi Kaur. You can also find it in Robert Frost, who sometimes inverts this tradition or renders it almost sinister: Frost's nostrum "I took the road less traveled by," for example, means almost the opposite of what most people who quote it think that it means, since within the poem there *is* no road less traveled, and the choice makes no difference: "The passing there / Had worn them really about the same." Frost's splendid, justly famous, and utterly terrifying late poem "Directive" appears to invite us to treat poetry like religion, the poet like a pastor or teacher. Frost's persona in that poem leads us "back out of all this now too much for us" to find the holy grail, the spirit of wholeness, in an abandoned childhood playhouse: "Drink and be whole again beyond confusion." And yet, in context, Frost may be inviting his readers to take their leave of this world: to get "beyond confusion," to drink from this cup, is simply to die (many Frost fans might disagree).

Read all the Frost you want—he's one of the greats—but please don't follow most of his advice, whether offered in character (as in "Mending Wall") or in his own tricky person. Walt Whitman and Emily Dickinson are better bets: both of those classic Americans understand that readers, in their day and afterward, might seek advice and wisdom from poems. Both poets torqued that desire by creating poems that show or suggest how life was and is more complex than any slogan would comprehend. "Whoever you are holding me now in hand," Whitman warned future readers, "I am not what you supposed, but far different." Dickinson, who sometimes did and sometimes did not want a reading public, certainly did not want to sound out loud and clear: "Tell all the truth but tell it slant," she advised, in a poem that goes on to compare "the Truth" (her capital letter) to lightning. She joins a host of poets who try at once to say what's true for all of us and to say something hard, or impossible, to articulate directly or in expository prose.

Poets who follow this pattern can be hard to understand because they want so hard to show you something that is inherently hard to say: if it were easy, they would use prose. Just as lyric poetry (sharing a part of the self) is not the opposite but the complement of poems of character (introducing you to someone else), wisdom and message and lesson are not the opposite but the complement of the weirdness that makes some poets so hard to understand, the weirdness we saw in chapter 4. We read such poets to learn, and perhaps to use in our own lives, their hard, weird truths. Jorie Graham's 1987 volume *The End of Beauty* taught a generation how to work crosscuts, self-interruptions, and puzzles from avant-garde film and French philosophy into American poems. The poems, as wholes, take a while to unpack, but their individual frames, their moments, have something to say straightaway: "A secret grows, a secret wants to be given away. / For a long time it swells and stains its bearer with beauty." That piece of wisdom, about what we know but can't say, what pleasures we cannot or do not communicate, comes from Graham's thirty-three-part poem (many of the parts are single lines) "Self-Portrait as the Gesture Between Them," about Adam and Eve. The book had a wide effect on other poets when it came out because it could be read as lyric, for its shared feeling, or for its personae, its distinctive characters, or for its intellectual challenge (how do those parts fit together?), or for its store of quotable advice.

Graham's juxtapositions are almost always serious. Other poets blend their wisdom with comedy, as when Jennifer Chang begins a poem:

It is not good to think
of everything as a mistake. I asked
for bacon in my sandwich, and then

I asked for more.

Was she wrong to ask for bacon? Or for more? These kinds of juxtapositions, which pit the general claim against the incongruous image, suggest the incomprehensibility, or the comedy, of life as lived, the inapplicability of so many general truths: they highlight moments when life seems hard to figure out.

No wonder we also find this kind of comedy—that is, this particular kind of wisdom, about how to live with absurdity—in poems written under, and against, authoritarian, censorious regimes. The Polish poet Ryszard Krynicki spent most of his writing life in Soviet-dominated late twentieth-century "People's Poland." His very short poems can address his own and other people's mental and practical resistance to censorship, and to Communist rule: "Poor moth, I can't help you, / I can only turn out the light." If Krynicki's figure (in the English translation by Stanislaw Baranczak and Clare Cavanagh) conveys any wisdom, it's not exactly by telling us what to do. Instead, the metaphor suggests, it's OK if nobody knows what to do, if you recognize—as any clearheaded observer would recognize—a drastic problem no one will soon solve. Poetry, since its language need not be literal, may specialize in problems that cannot be solved; sometimes it lets us lower our expectations, or live with partial failure, or recognize that what we want cannot be had. Consider this three-line poem (also translated by Cavanagh and Baranczak):

> You're all free—says the guard
> and the iron gate shuts
>
> this time from the other side.

Nobody wants to languish in prison. But (as in Hughes) the opposite of imprisonment, freedom, may not be what we think it is. Is all of Poland a prison? Is the whole world? Is adulthood? (What about parenthood, or a job?) What does it mean to call yourself free?

Then there are poets who run their advice for us through the fictional characters that they create. Louise Glück has been writing poems of wisdom, poems in which she and her readers learn something hard, almost throughout her writing life: some of her best-known poems begin with startling generalities, like the one (addressed to God, but also to parents and teachers) that opens her poem "Vita Nova": "You saved me; you should remember me." Her 2009 collection *A Village Life* departs from most of her earlier poems by taking place in a full-fledged fictional setting, vaguely Italian, far from any cultural center, inimical to ambition, and populated by characters who move in the course of the book from courtship to marriage to old age and death. One character advises another, early on, not to pursue ambition, not to leave their village:

> To my mind, you're better off if you stay;
> that way dreams don't damage you.
> At dusk, you sit by the window. Wherever you live,
> you can see the fields, the river, realities
> on which you cannot impose yourself—
>
> To me it's safe. The sun rises; the mist
> dissipates to reveal
> the immense mountain. You can see the peak,
> how white it is, even in summer.

Should we take these words as akin to Buddhist tranquility, nonattachment, enviable contentment with life as it is, where (at best) you can see its peaks from far away? Could they be Glück's own motto? Or do they portray a kind of resignation that we can and should reject? The carefully sketched scene raises those questions but leaves it up to you to answer them—after you've read the rest of the poem, or maybe Glück's whole book.

Other poets present themselves as trustworthy characters in their own poems: their personalities support their advice. Elizabeth Alexander's "Ars Poetica #100: I Believe" explains, and exemplifies, this kind of work: poetry for her (so she declares)

> is where we are ourselves
> (though Sterling Brown said
>
> "Every 'I' is a dramatic 'I'"),
> digging in the clam flats
>
> for the shell that snaps,
> emptying the proverbial pocketbook.

The poet and scholar Sterling Brown taught for decades at Howard University, the nation's flagship historically Black university, in DC, where Alexander grew up; he would be for her—as for many others—somebody to trust. She continues:

> Poetry (and now my voice is rising)
>
> is not all love, love, love,
> and I'm sorry the dog died.
>
> Poetry (here I hear myself loudest)
> is the human voice,
>
> and are we not of interest to each other?

Poetry is not always the human voice: we saw in chapter 4 poems that no one could read aloud. Poetry is not always any-thing except a name for a complicated history in which many people use words in many ways, making patterns that give readers and listeners pleasure, learning and changing many conventions and rules. Don't read poetry; read poems. But poetry for Alexander—the kind of poetry Alexander writes—always involves imagining people speaking, getting to know "one another"; and—as the friendly patience in Alexander's string of phrases implies—we get to know one another in ways that provide solidarity, that keep us from turning away or giving up on ourselves.

Nor does a poet have to speak directly to us, or to any audience, in order to offer wisdom through poems. There is an entire Renaissance genre of poems that purport to be, or consist of, their authors' last words, on a deathbed or before judicial execution. The English Catholic Chidiock Tichborne penned exactly one famous poem, in 1586, and it works just that way:

> My prime of youth is but a frost of cares,
> My feast of joy is but a dish of pain,
> My crop of corn is but a field of tares,
> And all my good is but vain hope of gain.
> The day is gone and yet I saw no sun,
> And now I live, and now my life is done.

"Corn," in an English poem, is likely wheat; "tares" are its harvested stalks. Time collapses around the man as he awaits execution: these balanced figures for worldly insignificance work almost equally well as a Christian prayer and as a model for other (say, Buddhist) resignation. Either way, they present themselves as models for us.

Yet poems of quotable wisdom need not stay solemn—
nor need they stop short. A. R. Ammons's book-length poem
Garbage (1993) begins as a meditation on a giant trash heap in
Florida and expands into a characteristically Ammons-y stack
of jokes, propositions, examples, counterexamples, and things
that remind him of things that remind him of things, with no
more (but no less) organization, perhaps, than a trash heap, or
a psyche:

> The heap of knickknacks (knickknackatery),
> whatnots (whatnotery), doodads, jews-harps,
>
> belt buckles, do-funnies, files, disks, pads,
> pesticide residues, nonprosodic high-tension
>
> lines, whimpering-wimp dolls, epichlorohydrin
> elastomotors, sulfur dioxide emissions, perfume
>
> sprays, radioactive williwaws: the people at
> Marine Shale are said to be "able to turn
>
> wastes into safe products": but some say these
> "products are themselves hazardous wastes":
>
> well what does anybody want: is there a world
> with no bitter aftertaste or post coital triste:
>
> what's a petit mort against a high moment:
> I mean, have you ever heard of such a thing:

Epichlorohydrin, an organic compound that smells like
garlic, is used to make resins and plastics; "post coital triste" refers
to "Triste est omne animal post coitum," a once-well-known

line from the Latin poet Ovid that means "After sex every animal is sad." "Nonprosodic" is a joke: either these "high-tension
/ lines" don't scan (they use free verse) or they are physical
metallic wires rather than lines of verse. Ammons turns his
catalog of items you might find in a hazardous-waste dump
into a celebration of American language, and then into an en-
vironmental lament, and then into a friendly comedian's shrug.
And in doing so he tosses up into the air, and then embeds or
questions or renders ironic, slogans you might apply to your
own life. Some solutions are part of the problem, and some
highs are worth the low. But some are not. To figure out which
proverb, which rules, should apply, you need judgment and
context; they are supplied in real life by friends, instincts, or
experience, and in Ammons by the rest of the poem.

Among all the poets of the twentieth century, Ammons
may well offer the highest number of pithy apothegms,
one-sentence claims about how we might live in general, and
also the greatest variety in ways to torque or skew them. A
bit later in *Garbage*, he admits (or brags): "I'm a goofball all
right, one of . . . the hurt, one of the criers, one of the shaken
/ lovers: if love were likely it would not be . . . love." The
independent clauses seem unrelated, though really the first
gives evidence for the second: if someone loves him, someone
might love you. His signature punctuation—always a colon,
never a period—became the sign of his provisional endings,
his sense that no single clause could wrap everything up.

To read *Garbage* straight through is to learn (by watching Ammons do it) how to keep your own mind in motion,
how to live with guesses and uncertainties, how not to stay

overwhelmed. He advises that we accept nothing as fixed, and nothing as final advice. And in his ongoing, rangy way, Ammons told us who he was and what he was doing:

> I want to see
>
> furrows of definition, both the centerings of
> furrow and the clumpy outcastings beyond: I do
>
> not want to be caught inside for clarity: I
> want clarity to be a smooth long bend
>
> disallowing no complexity in coming clean: why
> do I want this, complexity without confusion,
>
> clarity without confinement, time in time, not
> time splintered: if you are not gone at a certain
>
> age, your world is: or it is shriveled to a
> few people who know what you know

Ammons's meditations on what he really wants out of his own mental life, on "clarity," came to him not out of the blue but after contemplating his elderly father's infirmity. "Complexity without confusion," though, is something that anybody might want; poetry, with its ability to fold in colliding or overlapping simplicities, seems to Ammons like one way to get it. In this respect, Ammons keeps on suggesting, his poems are like life, where other poems—ones with strong closure, or no closure—may not be.

•

If you insist that poetry *has* to help people directly, that it *has* to offer advice or wisdom or a message you can distill for the AP exam, then you have excluded half the poems I like. You have also replicated the moralized strictures that make many students hate some of their English classes—the kind where every literary work must have a theme, a purpose, a message, a moral. These strictures make life especially hard for poets whose sense of right and wrong, and of who we are, runs counter to the received morality of their own time. That's one reason that so many modern gay poets, such as W. H. Auden and Hart Crane, learned to write in code, and one reason (there are others) why the history of same-sex love in literary writing has been so bound up with defenses of artistic license as something separate from morality, even with art for art's sake.

If you insist that poems should *not* help people directly, send a message, or offer advice, then you have excluded the other half of the poems I like, from the Psalms to Louise Glück. You have also prevented yourself from understanding, or coming to love, the great poems that intertwine their quotable wisdom with other kinds of effects. Sometimes those effects make the quotable wisdom ironic, as we saw in Frost, and in Yi-Sheng, and in chapter 2: Andrea del Sarto's exclamation "A man's reach should exceed his grasp / Or what's a heaven for?" means one thing on its own, something else when Browning's character seems to be making self-deluding excuses.

At other times, whatever else goes on around the poem—whatever delicacy or pathos or sublimity or intricacy or character work or difficulty or beauty—frames the wisdom as wiser still. By 1850 Alfred, Lord Tennyson had been writing and publishing poetry for twenty years, and working on a long poem in memory of his best friend for seventeen of those years. When that poem— *In Memoriam A.H.H.*—appeared in 1850, it gave him his lasting fame. The poem is a book-length lament in distinctive tetrameter quatrains for Arthur Henry Hallam, who died in 1833, age twenty-two. The first edition appeared in March 1850 with nothing to identify either the author or the dead person behind the initials; in September a reviewer identified Tennyson. By the end of that year he was Britain's poet laureate. The poem's 131 separable segments record Tennyson's grief, at first boundless, eventually contained, along with heartsick or resolute digressions on God and the absence of God, on weather and chance, on London, on the sea, on what we now call evolution ("nature red in tooth and claw"; *On the Origin of Species* had not yet appeared), and on the future of civilization. Some segments present pure scenes of deprivation, like segment VII, where Tennyson walks, almost sleepwalks, to Hallam's onetime address:

> Dark house, by which once more I stand
>   Here in the long unlovely street,
>   Doors, where my heart was used to beat
> So quickly, waiting for a hand,
>
> A hand that can be clasp'd no more—
>   Behold me, for I cannot sleep,
>   And like a guilty thing I creep
> At earliest morning to the door.

He is not here; but far away
>The noise of life begins again,
>And ghastly thro' the drizzling rain
On the bald street breaks the blank day.

Tennyson waits six lines for the main verb, as if waiting for the dam to break, so that he can then take his futile walk to the door where his best friend once lived. Such raw and embodied feeling between men now reads (perhaps anachronistically) as homoerotic: Tennyson has lost his first, best love. *Love*, the word, resounds through the poem. And love, erotic or otherwise, entails a kind of loyalty stronger than anything to which we could compare it, an attachment that may be exclusive or otherwise (Hallam was engaged to Tennyson's sister), a bond that makes life worthwhile, whatever happens afterward.

You can read the poem, and love the poem, and the book-length sequence to which it belongs, in the ways I brought up in chapters 1 and 2: as a way to put feelings in words and as a portrait of a particular man in his grief. But you can also read it—and Victorian Tennyson fans very much did read it—as a way to share advice, to show by example what a man consumed by grief can and should do. You may recognize the conclusion to segment XXVII, one of the first parts of *In Memoriam* that Tennyson composed:

I envy not in any moods
>The captive void of noble rage,
>The linnet born within the cage,
That never knew the summer woods:

I envy not the beast that takes
   His license in the field of time,
   Unfetter'd by the sense of crime,
To whom a conscience never wakes;

Nor, what may count itself as blest,
   The heart that never plighted troth
   But stagnates in the weeds of sloth;
Nor any want-begotten rest.

I hold it true, whate'er befall;
   I feel it, when I sorrow most;
   'Tis better to have loved and lost
Than never to have loved at all.

Those aching quatrains, with their slightly stagy compar-isons, work hard to bring you to a claim that Tennyson seems to want you, too, to accept: giving someone your heart, or trusting a friend absolutely, is better than not doing those things, even though you may not get to keep what you have. Indeed, you cannot keep anything forever: not a house, not a friend, not a lover, not an idea, not a cent. Everything passes and everyone dies. You can use this same truth (as Tichborne did, as Ecclesiastes does) to advocate detachment from things of this world, or (as Shakespeare does in Sonnet 73) "to make thy love more strong." Tennyson has rephrased the latter sen-timent as direct advice, to you and to himself. He has also set the claim amid binary contrasts, telling his own grieving self that he would prefer *not* to be a series of things: a prisoner who never gets angry, a caged bird who has never flown or sung free, a beast without conscience, a person too lazy to fall in love.

In saying so he has likened himself to the opposite of each thing: a prisoner who *is* angry; a beast who has experienced consciousness; a caged bird who *has* flown free, and perhaps known a mate. And in telling us that he would rather be who he is, feel as he does, than go without the pain that he now feels, he builds up to another line of detachable, quotable wisdom, one often used in ways that subtract half its force. "'Tis better to have loved and lost" means not just that it's better to date and break up than never to date (though that too) but that commitment beats pusillanimity; risk aversion is no way to live. This claim has, moreover, the force of a religious credo: "I hold it true, whate'er befall." He holds himself up as a kind of proof by least likely case, since he seems peculiarly unlikely to sustain this belief, having already lost so much.

Victorians treasured *In Memoriam* not just for its depictions of grief, its defenses of love, but for its picture of gradual, respectful recovery. They wanted the poem to give them a good cry, then show, and tell, them how they might stop sulking and go on. (Queen Victoria, who lost her husband in 1861, told Tennyson, "Next to the Bible *In Memoriam* is my comfort.") Some of the parts of the book take on a liturgical quality; you might repeat them quietly to yourself.

> I wage not any feud with Death
>   For changes wrought on form and face;
>   No lower life that earth's embrace
> May breed with him, can fright my faith.

Eternal process moving on,
    From state to state the spirit walks;
    And these are but the shatter'd stalks,
Or ruin'd chrysalis of one.

Nor blame I Death, because he bare
    The use of virtue out of earth:
    I know transplanted human worth
Will bloom to profit, otherwhere.

For this alone on Death I wreak
    The wrath that garners in my heart;
    He put our lives so far apart
We cannot hear each other speak.

That's segment LXXXII. You do not have to choose between consolation and grief; you can admit both, in yourself
and in your surviving friends and in whatever faith you sustain. For Tennyson, both nature and people are getting better,
all part of one "eternal process," from the potential for new
romantic love to the emergence of worms after rain. You can
hold that belief (which makes death ultimately impotent) and
yet still feel alone: civilization may improve all of us, but Hallam will never come back to him. Part of the power that builds
up throughout the long poem comes from its message—and
it is a message—that you do not have to forget your lost love,
nor stop speaking about that love, in order to love again.

    There is no bright line—some would say no line at all—
between what a poem wants to say and what a poem tries to
do, between what a poem has to tell you and how it wants
(if it wants at all) to help you. Not only the literal advice we

find in so many poems but also the governing metaphors can work as promises, as means of solidarity, so that the poem makes itself available for your use, if not like a lover then like a friend, or a trail guide, or a pocketknife. Carmen Giménez Smith's "Tree Tree Tree" not only promises to help you, to stand with you in solidarity, but tells you—at the very end— what it is doing. Smith remembers the childhood game of "repeating a word until it ceases to mean,"

> as if leaves and leaves and green and trunk
> were not the end of this tree.
>
> Meanwhile there is the ring in our ears, and
>
> tree and tree have become a forest.
> Trees give nothing, not even a sound.
>
> Our tongues make branches move.

Giménez Smith has written a compact poem, one metaphor, several long *e* sounds, and nine lines long, about the power of speaking up: if a tree falls in the forest and we see something, we should say so.

That kind of advice (however indirect) has ethical burdens and shared futures in mind, even though it does not instruct us directly (as Tennyson did) about what to believe, what to do. Other poems of instruction work through irony, even through discouragement: A. E. Housman, in a famous poem beginning "Terence, this is stupid stuff," explains that he wants his own poems not to justify the world as it is, nor exactly to delight us (beer "does more than Milton can / To justify God's ways to man"), but to work as a kind of vaccine for the pain in the world, a low dose of poison that lets us survive the higher doses real life always brings. An extraordinarily famous Renaissance poem by Thomas Nashe, usually given the title "A Litany in Time of Plague" (though Nashe never gave it that title), modulates from individual sadnesses into a shared chant, a funeral service, a resignation to what God may have in store. One of its six stanzas says:

Beauty is but a flower
Which wrinkles will devour;
Brightness falls from the air;
Queens have died young and fair;
Dust hath closed Helen's eye.
I am sick, I must die.
Lord, have mercy on us!

Nashe borrows the form and some of the words from psalms and prayers his first readers would have heard often in church. The effect is incantatory, as if to chant away doubt, fear, and any hope of resistance to God's will. ("Brightness falls from the air" would later furnish a title for the great science fiction writer James Tiptree Jr.)

If you believe that tragedy is the highest form of literature and resignation the highest form of wisdom, then poems like Nashe's might be your favorites. If—like Adrienne Rich— you hold otherwise, you might want poems whose wisdom helps you and others get what you have never had, or work together for social and personal change. You might—as you survey the literary past— treasure sterling abolitionist poems like Longfellow's "The Warning," or poems defending a nation of immigrants, like Emma Lazarus's "The New Colossus," or poems like Sterling Brown's about racial justice, directed first—if not only—to Black readers (a good place to start is "Slim in Atlanta").You might also want poems that advise radicals and conservatives to hear one another and whose style demonstrates that kind of patience; try Richard Wilbur's terrific and too-little-known stanzaic poem "For the Student Strikers," if that is the kind of poem you think we need.

That is to say, you can go to poems not just for advice about your own life but for advice about public life too, and about your own role in a wider struggle. That advice can exhort, or encourage, or ask you to think before you act. Poets may struggle to frame their advice, their wisdom, their words for your use; they may also, when asked, refuse to provide them. Soon after the First World War began, W. B. Yeats, already famous in Britain and Ireland (where feelings about the war were very mixed), was asked to write in support of neutral nations. He answered, in 1915:

> I think it better that in times like these
> A poet keep his mouth shut, for in truth
> We have no gift to set a statesman right;
> He's had enough of meddling who can please
> A young girl in the indolence of her youth,
> Or an old man upon a winter's night.

(The poem changed titles and details several times; the final version bore the title "On Being Asked for a War Poem.")

The composition of poetry is "meddling"; it carries no wisdom and aims, at best, to "please." And yet, before and after 1915, Yeats often tried in verse to set statesmen right, worrying, for example, about the aftermath of the Easter Rising, in durable, tormented, ambivalent trimeters published under the title "Easter 1916." Were the Irish rebels and martyrs, with their stony resolve, their "hearts with one purpose alone," deplorable or admirable or both? Would their sacrifice, with its "terrible beauty," achieve the independence for which they worked or lead to bloodshed not worth what it cost? Wisdom, there, meant letting his uncertainties show; it also meant not publishing the poem in question for more than three years after he had written it and shown it to his friends.

Then there are poets whose wisdom, whose advice, urges us to take collective action. Though her poems never sound like "The New Colossus," nor like a modern political speech, Natalie Eilbert, no less than Rich, has to be called a poet of action or of activism, one who wants her poems to help real people change the real world, the world outside our psyches as well as within them. She might be called a poet of the Me Too movement, the vigorous public attempt, beginning in late 2017, to make clear the ubiquity and the invidiousness of sexual harassment and sexual assault, and then to do something about it. The title for Eilbert's book-length poem *Indictus* (2018), a play on Henley's "Invictus," could mean "indict us" (bring criminal charges against us) or "unsung, untold, unheard, unsaid" (Latin *in*, for "not," plus *dictus*). The volume begins with a kind of spell, a way to use words that gather and hold power. Eilbert writes, in mingled verse and prose:

I envision a world where the men are gone who pulled language out of my mouth to push themselves in.

Men who said what I could not speak.

I push language back into the body I could never save— and I pull from the hole a roster.

Eilbert belongs not just to a Me Too moment, not just to the legacy of Adrienne Rich, Audre Lorde, and other poets and essayists back through the 1960s, but also to the far longer tradition—going back to the biblical Jonah and Jeremiah— of poems as actions, poems as words of power, poems whose arrangements try to do something to the rest of the world: a blessing, a spell, a prayer, a curse, a warning, a sermon.

We have seen poems that work both as lyrics (embodied, enacted feeling) and as depictions of characters. We have seen poems that work both as lyrics and as displays of technique, almost like magic (such as Keats's "Ode to a Nightingale"). Eilbert's book-length poem works at once as practical advice, as words that many of us need to hear for moral and practical reasons, and as a kind of ineffable, protective spell, asserting its supernatural or (with apologies to Matthew Arnold) quasi-religious force. Eilbert's pages do not just work *like* protective magic; they tell us, at times, that they *are* magic, weaving counterspells against sexual mistreatment and defending a community, like the Golem of Prague:

A rock beneath my feet grows new rhetoric.
I am golem I am clay I am
the breath of my own shitty god....

I want to be the name men call to scatter their ashes.
I want to be the name
they can't close their eyes against.

No wonder she uses the present tense so often, since the problem is here and now: "*What else can I defile? I ask, as I wipe my chin against my elders.*" Wisdom here lies in seeing, and in knowing how to see, that something has to be done: not just to change the law but to change the language, to change our states of mind.

I am going out of my way to call attention to Eilbert's book here not just because I like it a lot but because it is, literally, exemplary of our moment, a moment when readers seem to want both wisdom—messages—and outrage from literature of any kind, and from poems in particular. Wisdom and outrage can accompany, rather than substituting for, feelings, character, technique. These desiderata are not the same: you can get one thing from one poem without demanding all the rest! But they may be connected: seeing your own life reflected in someone else's experience, after all, is the literal origin of the phrase "me too." And Eilbert does not stand alone. Her poetry tries to become, to call into being, a kind of avenger, a righteous successor to Sylvia Plath's reckless Lady Lazarus, who announces momentously, "I eat men like air." And the point of Plath's poem "Lady Lazarus" is not the suicide but the resurrection: the voice of the poem comes back to defend the poet, and perhaps to defend all women—the language has to be internally violent, excessive, jarring. Otherwise it could not defend her effectively against the violence outside. Eilbert moves in similar directions:

Consent is a hole I've dropped all silverware through. I eat
   with arms
tied. I began this by pronouncing God into the silk of a
   wound

when I fondled commandment into an act of mercy. It was
   no big deal—
it was already there. I simply found a messiah and polluted
   the air

with my kind.

The worse the world looks, the more urgent action seems,
the less interested you might be in reading or writing poems
that lack a message, that do not try to make anything practical
or concrete or socially visible happen. Call it the *Casablanca*
problem: the feelings and the problems of three little people don't amount to a hill of beans in this crazy world, even
if the people are John Donne, Emily Dickinson, and Marianne Moore. But this same crazy world makes it hard to calm
down, hard to step back, and hard to decide what to do: the
same unrelenting headlines that make lyric poetry, for some
of us, less appealing on certain days might make the poetry of
wisdom, of advice, of how to act rightly, more so.

   And that poetry includes not only hortatory verse, verse
that tells you directly what you ought to do, but also exemplary verse of public frustration, explosive and revelatory
verse like Eilbert's, even sarcastic political poems like W. S.
Merwin's "For a Coming Extinction," addressed to a gray
whale and ending bitterly, "Tell them / That it is we who are
important." The poetry of effective wisdom has to include a

very large range of tones, not only the earnest and the harsh but the wryly fed-up, the roiling, the grim, the nearly comic, and the gently exasperated, like Langston Hughes's "Tired," much circulated online in 2018, in which the poet says he is "tired of waiting" for the world to change on its own.

Such poets as Eilbert, or Hughes, or the Yeats of "Easter 1916," do not just have something to say, some wisdom about what you can or should do; they have some sense of who's listening, whom they address. When you think about poets speaking to themselves, or to nobody, or to God, or to their closest friends, you can often envision them in private. When you think about poets before an imagined public, before multiple listeners, or within the course of history—the history that Yeats compared to a "living stream"—you have to think about who that public could be, where it comes from, what it expects. Thus far we have been thinking about single readers (however removed in time or space), and about poets who seem to write for themselves. How do entire communities use poems? How do we know? How can we know?

chapter six

COMMUNITY

SOME POEMS SEEM PRIVATE: READING THEM FEELS ALMOST like eavesdropping. "I'm Nobody—who are you? / Are you—Nobody—too?" asks Emily Dickinson, imagining her own poems as part of a secret or imaginary community. And yet even Dickinson (who sent many of her poems to friends, in letters) imagined a set of real people who would read her work. Other poets, and readers, seek larger, more public communities; they want sets of readers who share some strand of history, or some public affiliation, or some common cause. We have seen, over five chapters and several millennia of poems, how poems can engage and delight readers one at a time; chapter 5 showed how some poems and poets encourage individual readers to take action, to do things. This final chapter will move the camera back, expand the view, and see how poems can address, imagine, and even call into being versions of community, showing what holds groups of people together and how some poems speak to many people at once.

Most of this book so far has introduced you to poems by showing you how I read them, or why I like them, or what the poets say they want to do (even when—as with Eilbert, or Oliver Goldsmith, or Urayoán Noël) what they want to do involves social change. This chapter first departs from that procedure by showing you historical evidence about how real readers and listeners and audiences and fans (not just me) have found community through poems. I'll look then at poems that speak directly to national, regional, ethnic, and professional identities: most of my favorites acknowledge more than one identity at once. We'll see a few poems from centuries past with directly political goals (we have already seen a few from our own day), and then look at poems that try to address everybody, to imagine a common human community. We'll see a couple of twentieth-century poets who changed their styles and goals entirely—and produced their best work—when, and because, they changed their ideas about who they were writing for and what kinds of persons they hoped to reach. This chapter—and this book—then come to an end with two more of my own favorite poems, showing not single reasons to read single poems but rather how one poem can reach many readers in many ways.

•

We have already seen how some poets try to, or want to, cause their readers to take action in public, in concert. You might wonder whether those poets succeed, and what counts as success. You might also wonder how we know. One answer is that as a reader of poetry, I do not want that question to even arise: whether you care for a poem, or a song, or a person, should not depend on how influential that poem, or song, or person has already been. You don't choose your friends on the basis of their existing influence or popularity; why should you choose your favorite poems that way?

But there are other answers. At many junctures, small and large, in many slices of history—and within American history alone—poems have brought people together, and scholars have gathered evidence that they did, and still do. Some of those poems guided social movements, changed public policy, helped or hurt people in very practical ways, while others simply spoke to some aspect of life that many, many people in, say, 1950s Iowa or 1870s New England or 2010s internet culture shared. Some poems bring people together around the shared identity of anxious youth: that's just as true for Allen Ginsberg's *Howl*—subject of a famous obscenity trial and a book that sold almost one million copies before the poet's death in 1997—as for Rupi Kaur's best-selling short poems today. Critics who dislike those poems, or—worse yet—make fun of them are simply not their audience, nor is their kind of popularity new. The historian Joan Shelley Rubin has shown how many published American poems found their way into grade schools, high schools, Boy Scout and Girl Scout troops, and into Jewish and Christian liturgies during the first half of the twentieth century: the practice of reciting poems aloud before a school-age audience, Rubin concludes, and the memorization that the recitals required, "furnished the opportunity, long after graduation, for social exchange on the basis of shared experience," much as we quote pop lyrics to one another now.

Another scholar, Mike Chasar, has studied the journal-keeping and scrapbooking practices of twentieth-century

Americans. One scrapbook presents poems by "Emily Dickinson" and "modernist writing by Ezra Pound, Stephen Crane, H.D. . . . alongside popular verse . . . like 'Loneliness,' 'My Love for You' and 'What Are the Waves Saying?.'" Chasar has also unearthed the archives of a 1930s radio show consisting largely of poems read over the airwaves: at one point the program got "upwards of twenty thousand fan letters per month." Urayoán Noel, whose verse we saw in chapter 3, has looked at the practice of writing, and sharing, and performing poetry in New York's Puerto Rican communities from the 1970s to the present. Some of these poets and poems, and one of their venues—the Nuyorican Poets Café—took part in the national upsurge of interest in poets' live performance during the 1990s. Others (such as Jorge Brandon, nicknamed "El Coco Que Habla," "the Speaking Coconut") never published their poems; they were known for their readings among other Nuyorican writers and left the scene before cameras arrived.

Such evidence of popular poetry, of poetry to which many people responded, of poetry that brought people together, can be found—once you start looking—in every generation of American life, from the manuscript circulation of poems about the American Revolution not long after the revolution, to the public success of Henry Wadsworth Longfellow, to the present-day Favorite Poem Project online, to the innumerable poems quoted and shared, in part or in whole, on Tumblr and other social media. And that is to say nothing of the individual poems that have become irreplaceable in US civic life: the sonnet by Emma Lazarus, for example, engraved on the base of the Statue of Liberty, declaring this country to be a nation of immigrants: "I lift my lamp beside the golden door!"

I take American poets for most of my examples because I am writing in the United States, but of course other nations have at least equally salient poets and poems, from Adam Mickiewicz in nineteenth-century Poland to Louise Bennett in Jamaica, who read her poems on the radio (she was also a radio host) during the early years of Jamaican independence; few writers, few voices, in Jamaica were more widely recognized. In pre-Islamic Arabic, in Homeric Greece, in early medieval Ireland, in modern bars and auditoriums, entire forms of poetry could or can rely on audience response: the earliest Arabic-language poetry, for example (in the words of the scholar and translator James Montgomery) "is addressed to, and entirely dependent upon, a group of listeners; it appeals to others and voices challenges to them" (compare modern rap battles). Even within modern European languages and their page-based traditions, poems written, copied, exchanged, memorized, and recited on formal occasions provide a basis for community, for solidarity, in nations, in ethnic groups, in fandoms, and in officially certified professions. Rudyard Kipling's 1907 poem "The Sons of Martha" speaks for the people who fix machines, who make networks run, who provide what we now know as infrastructure repair, routine maintenance, and tech support:

> It is their care in all the ages to take the buffet and cushion
>   the shock.
> It is their care that the gear engages; it is their care that the
>   switches lock.
> It is their care that the wheels run truly; it is their care to
>   embark and entrain,

Tally, transport, and deliver duly the Sons of Mary by
    land and main.

They do not preach that their God will rouse them a little
    before the nuts work loose.
They do not teach that His Pity allows them to leave their
    job when they damn-well choose.
As in the thronged and the lighted ways, so in the dark and
    the desert they stand,
Wary and watchful all their days that their brethren's days
    may be long in the land.

Inspired by "The Sons of Martha," a Canadian engineering professor in 1922 asked Kipling to devise a ritual for the professional induction ("calling") of engineers: Kipling complied, producing the ceremony of the Iron Ring, still used today.

Such poems' presence in modern communal life, their ability to bring readers and audiences together, is not mere conjecture or wish on the part of the poet, nor of the poet's hopeful handful of readers, but documented public fact. They may not be your favorite poems, or mine, but their existence should not be denied; nor should the present-day wealth of opportunities to hear and perform poetry off the printed page, from famous single venues such as Chicago's Green Mill (where the poetry slam was apparently invented) and the Nuyorican Poets Café to the national competitions of today, whose entrants and winners have, in the present century, made clear their ability to generate poems that also work on the page.

That said: I have been trying to write, not a book about what poems are already popular, nor a book about how to see live performances and audiences, but rather a book that helps you, "a single separate person" (in Whitman's words), navigate the variety of poems and kinds of poems you might want to read. Some of those poems—but only some of them—speak to the public life, to the sense of community, that other poems (like Longfellow's and Bennett's) have in fact achieved.

We saw, in chapter 1, poems written in prisons, where literal imprisonment also stands for the single body, the separate self. But prisons are part of a state, and a system, and a set of communities, as well. Modern American poets writing from, or about, the carceral system often look back to Etheridge Knight's *Poems from Prison* (1968), in which Knight imagines both a cast of characters around him (as in his often-anthologized "Hard Rock Returns to Prison from the Hospital for the Criminally Insane") and a community far beyond the prison, as in "The Idea of Ancestry." "Taped to the wall of my cell are 47 pictures: 47 black / faces," the latter poem begins. "I am all of them, they are all of me; / they are farmers, I am a thief, I am me, they are thee." Knight's sense of himself—as Terrance Hayes emphasizes in Hayes's 2018 book about Knight—emerges from a collective identity that extends back in time as well as past the prison walls: "Each fall the graves of my grandfathers call me," Knight goes on. "This yr there is a gray stone wall damming my stream."

When we think about a large, coherent community with its own traditions of art, and language, and culture, its own kinship and fellowship, many of us are likely to think of a nation. Writers in the United States, Poland, Ireland, Jamaica, post-apartheid South Africa, and many other countries—whether or not they became famous for doing it—have used poetry to imagine, celebrate, or help fight for the better nation they wanted to see, and to define that nation for its members. Walt Whitman announced in 1855, "The Americans of all nations at any time upon the earth, have probably the fullest poetical nature. The United States themselves are essentially the greatest poem." Most of my favorite poems addressed to some particular group of people (Whitman's among them) speak to more than one group: the nation is never all they have in mind. We've already seen these effects at work in Whitman, who wants to speak to *you*, personally, and also to Americans in general, and to everyone at once, and as well to particular soldiers, and mothers, and teachers, and streetcar conductors. But these goals are hardly unique to Whitman or the United States. Consider a poet as quiet as Whitman is loud, Bill Manhire, the author of "Milky Way Bar":

> I live at the edge of the universe,
> like everybody else. Sometimes I think
> congratulations are in order:
> I look out at the stars
> and my eye merely blinks a little,
> my voice settles for a sigh.
>
> But my whole pleasure is the inconspicuous;
> I love the unimportant thing.
> I go down to the Twilight Arcade
> and watch the Martian invaders,
> already appalled by our language,
> pointing at what they want.

This poem works one way if you're reading it in the United States, where it could be about anybody at all or about a personality type; we all live in the same galaxy, on a blue planet near the edge of one spiral arm. It reads another way if you are, like Manhire, a citizen of New Zealand/Aotearoa, a small, remote, relatively peaceful country of islands whose wry collective self-image fits the comic turn in the opening line. To live in New Zealand—Manhire suggests—is to feel marginal; but in another sense, isn't everyone marginal? How many people, even in Beijing or London, end up central to the history of the world? Accept the way that we all live "at the edge of the universe," on the other hand, accept your distance from the famous stars, and you can try to make yourself and your friends, or your seaside town, or your small country, your own center of being.

That kind of confident understatement—that refusal to raise one's voice, that quiet sense that things are OK here—also looks like a national characteristic, at least to one kind of New Zealand Pākehā ("white") self-conception. Yet New Zealand—like the United States—was what historians call a white settler colony: Europeans founded the modern country by displacing non-European peoples who already lived there, and who of course still do. (A later New Zealand poet, Tayi Tibble, calls the day of the treaty that founded the country "the anniversary / of the greatest failed marriage this nation has ever seen.") Manhire's short poem does not delve into that history, but he does imagine louder invaders on the beaches, "appalled by our language," which they may not speak, interested only in "what they want." Manhire has made a poem about national identity that aspires, ironically, to universality, to portray someone who feels "like everybody else," and also a poem that wonders whether we will ever be, to some on-coming future, almost as the European settlers were to tangata whenua (Māori people) not so long ago.

You can find similar multiple dimensions, ways of speaking to multiple communities (only some of which include the poet), in poems that feel nothing like Manhire's and have nothing to do with New Zealand. Juan Felipe Herrera's signature poem "Punk Half Panther" announces—accurately enough—that he will defend and celebrate young Chicanx people (men, mostly) and their souped-up cars. Here is just the first part of that poem:

Lissen
to the whistle of night bats—
oye como va,
in the engines, in the Chevys
& armed Impalas, the Toyota gangsta'
monsters, surf of new world colony definitions
& quasars & culture prostars going blam

   over the Mpire, the once-Mpire, carcass
neural desires for the Nothing. i amble
outside the Goddess mountain. Cut across
the San Joaquín Valley, Santiago de Cuba,
Thailand & Yevtushenko's stations;
hunched humans snap off cotton heads
gone awry & twist
nuclear vine legs.

Jut out to sea, once again—this slip
sidewalk of impossible migrations. Poesy mad
& Chicano-style undone wild.

"*Oye como va*" ("hear how it goes," "how's it going?") refers to a 1970 radio hit by the band Santana, and also ad-
monishes us to listen, "lissen," to the drivers and to their cars.
Herrera imagines not just the sea of young riders, like ex-
ploding stars, but also an intercontinental network of young
people, of talkers, of writers, so excited that it seems like they
will explode, so sped-up that they leave letters out of their
words, a network that somehow responds to the global peril
of nuclear weapons, matching the urgency of our potential
destruction. Its "impossible migrations" are "Chicano-style,"
but not *only* Chicano; these migrations cover the entire one-
time American "Mpire" and could take place in Thailand too.
"Cotton heads / gone awry" are bolls of picked cotton, but
they're also white-haired elders baffled by new styles, styles
that ask us to run with them (if we can keep up), to follow
them (though we might lose track), to identify them at once
with a particular ethnic group and with a spirit of almost ni-
hilistic, unquenchable, picaresque desire that also happens to
be the emblem of a nation within a nation.

The political thinker Benedict Anderson made waves in
the 1980s with a book called *Imagined Communities*: Anderson
showed lay readers—and reminded experts—that nations are
not natural objects, like grains of sand or pieces of paper,
nor yet matters of force and law alone, but also creations
of habit and culture, imagined into being by their citizens

or would-be citizens. Anderson explained how nineteenth-
century writers, and especially nineteenth-century newspapers, brought nations into being, showing (for example)
Polish speakers in Russian territory how to see themselves
as Poles. This process can work, and has worked, through poetry too. It can work in reverse, complicating rather than
reinforcing a group identity, as when poets like Czeslaw
Milosz and Wisława Szymborska in Polish, Elizabeth Bishop
and Paul Muldoon in English, write against narrow, exclu-
sionary nationalisms. It can encourage or discourage revolutions, as well as exhort (or impede) political activity in
peacetime, not just by people who have or want a nation but
also by other groups that demand recognition. Often these
poems were turned into songs or chants; some of them sound
pretty flat when they're read without the music long after
the fact. Others, though, hold up well, especially when they
leave space for those mixed feelings that Auden defined as
the essence of genuine poems: take "Easter 1916" (discussed
in chapter 5). Or take the Singaporean poet Arthur Yap's am-
bivalence about the rapid growth of his own nation, where
"one urban expansion / has to lean on another / or they die."

All these poems also address a longer history—going
back to the Hebrew Bible, to Exodus, to Jeremiah—in which
some poets expect to speak to a public, in a timely fashion,
about public events. If you know William Wordsworth only
as a Romantic poet who loved daffodils and childhood, and
John Milton only as the polymathic author of *Paradise Lost*,
you might be surprised to encounter William Wordsworth's
sonnet "London, 1802":

Milton! thou shouldst be living at this hour:
England hath need of thee: she is a fen
Of stagnant waters: altar, sword, and pen,
Fireside, the heroic wealth of hall and bower,
Have forfeited their ancient English dower
Of inward happiness. We are selfish men;
Oh! raise us up, return to us again;
And give us manners, virtue, freedom, power.
Thy soul was like a Star, and dwelt apart:
Thou hadst a voice whose sound was like the sea:
Pure as the naked heavens, majestic, free,
So didst thou travel on life's common way,
In cheerful godliness; and yet thy heart
The lowliest duties on herself did lay.

Milton supported the parliamentary side against King
Charles I in the English civil wars of the 1640s and wrote at
length in defense of the victors' unpopular decision to behead
the king. He served as Latin secretary under the revolutionary
ruler Oliver Cromwell and was almost executed for treason
after the monarchy returned. If you go looking (and you need
not look hard), you can find traces of Milton's radical politics
all over his greatest poems, where the only legitimate mon-
arch is God. Yet eighteenth-century poets, who usually revered
or imitated Milton's majestic verse, often put his politics to
one side.

Not Wordsworth (or not the young Wordsworth, anyway),
for whom Milton comes to bring not a style but a sword.
Milton also gives Wordsworth examples of self-confidence,

dignity, and even humility, since a man who could have spent his whole life writing poetry instead spent dutiful years in service to his nation, composing and supervising diplomatic and bureaucratic prose. Radicals in politics sometimes get accused of disregarding the past; part of the point of this sonnet (itself, *as* a sonnet, a formal link back to the past) is to establish that England's past *is* radical, that beyond the reaction and self-enrichment that dominated the news of 1802 lies a long-sufficient, deeply English example.

Except that Wordsworth is not, exactly, radical: What does he want the nation, his nation, Milton's nation, the English nation, to do? How does he feel about the 1802 Treaty of Amiens, a kind of pause button in the Napoleonic Wars? Or about kings (Milton was not a fan)? It's not clear from the sonnet alone; what's clear is that Wordsworth wants England and English citizens to act bravely and honestly, unswayed by commercial interests, and to see themselves as the rightful inheritors of the epic poet who now rests, or travels, above us, a guiding star.

Other poets and poems—even long ago—have taken clearer sides. Oliver Goldsmith's elegant, passionate, once ultra-popular "The Deserted Village" (1770) addresses the decline of rural life in Britain, as farmers and their children head for cities and their land—once held in common or worked for subsistence—becomes the property of large estates. "The Deserted Village" presents poverty and dispossession; a once-self-sufficient locality crushed by the exigencies of international trade; the cordoning off of a public good for private use; the end of a culture in which rich people felt responsible for and to the poor (think *Downton Abbey*); and that culture's replacement by short-sighted urban greed. Goldsmith's stately couplets contain their own brakes, their own checks and balances (as Americans say) on what would otherwise sound like a rant, as Goldsmith addresses the village itself:

> Sunk are thy bowers, in shapeless ruin all,
> And the long grass o'ertops the mouldering wall;
> And, trembling, shrinking from the spoiler's hand,
> Far, far away, thy children leave the land.
> Ill fares the land, to hastening ills a prey,
> Where wealth accumulates, and men decay:
> Princes and lords may flourish, or may fade;
> A breath can make them, as a breath has made;
> But a bold peasantry, their country's pride,
> When once destroyed, can never be supplied.

Can England (or Ireland, where Goldsmith grew up) dig itself out of such a hole? The real dignity of the nation rests not in palaces, not in any one person, but in local customs and broader social norms, which support their inhabitants almost as the carefully matched pairs of nouns support one another in Goldsmith's lines, some of the last great balanced eighteenth-century couplets before the form concluded its classic run. No time and place is exactly like any other, but if you think about closed stores on small-town Main Streets and Walmarts paying minimum wage a mile away, you'll come pretty close to Goldsmith's village; no wonder the left-wing social critic Tony Judt used *Ill Fares the Land* as the title for his penultimate book.

These poets spoke to traditions in which communities like theirs—the English village, or the English nation—had already been represented. What if you feel that your community has never been represented in verse, or that it has not been represented well? You might decide to represent it yourself: so many styles and kinds of poems (including Herrera's) come from a poet's decision to bring into poetry a set of people, a way of using language, even a kind of geographical space, that has not yet been represented adequately. The efforts of Derek Walcott, Vahni Capildeo, and others to make the modes of English seasonal lyric poetry fit West Indian seasons—not spring-summer-autumn but rainy-and-dry, or balmy-and-hurricane—make vivid examples.

But they are hardly the only ones. Lorine Niedecker, the Wisconsin modernist whom we met in chapter 3, called her first book *New Goose* (1946) in part because she saw its rhyming stanzas as revisions of the English Mother Goose. Niedecker's poems—often short, with rich acoustic patterns despite their simple vocabulary—mix elegance with deprivation, dissatisfaction with careful making-do. They represent her resource-poor Wisconsinites, who are like her extended family:

> The clothesline post is set
> yet no totem-carvings distinguish the Niedecker tribe
> from the rest; every seventh day they wash:
> worship sun; fear rain, their neighbors' eyes;
> raise their hands from ground to sky,
> and hang or fall by the whiteness of their all.

Words in such poems can seem to huddle together, to crowd each other, as the people do, whether they are an extended family, or a town, or a "tribe." The single stanza's aurally satisfying closure matches the much less satisfying bounds and fences of Niedecker's whole "tribe," and of the town that may judge them on the basis of whether they, and their laundry, stay clean, and perhaps racially white.

Niedecker was hardly the only American poet whose style seemed part and parcel of her attention to locale, to groups of people in place. C. D. Wright continued to draw on her Ozark heritage even as she spent much of her life in Rhode Island. Wright's last book, *ShallCross* (2017), includes very long lists, very short lyrics, fragments of stories, responses to visual art, and attention to the tough and sometimes self-destructive lives of other artists, as in the foldout catalog poem "The Obscure Lives of the Poets," or in the title poem, a lament for the Georgia-based singer and songwriter Vic Chesnutt:

> Now who will make the record of us
> Who will be the author
> Of our blind and bilious hours
> Of the silken ear of our years.

Wright, too, stayed alert to multiple communities; part of her genius involved the way she drew on the particular language, the sociolects and idiolects, that they used. Her "we" can mean herself plus others from her Ozark background, herself plus other artists, or herself plus you, the individual reader, in a group of two. "Poem Without Angel Food" invokes a "we" who are also an "I" who are also a family who are also southern who are also a body of readers:

> Well, a great many things have been said
> in the oven of hours. We have not been
> shaken out of the magnolias. Today was another
> hard day. And tomorrow will be harder. Well,
> that sounds like our gong. But we'll have
> the boy's birthday and we will have
> music and cake. Well, I will think only
> good thoughts and go up and talk to the rock.

The poem is at once a celebration and an invitation. We overhear the speech of hardworking, well-meaning Americans, probably southern and probably parents and probably older than many of Wright's readers now. They plan (or she plans) a party for the next day to celebrate children, without "angel food," meaning both that their food is nothing fancy and that they eat only food fit for homely human beings. If you are the sort of reader who wants to connect new poems to the poetic past, you might notice how Wright skirts, but never entirely flees, familiar iambic pentameter patterns, like those we have just heard in Wordsworth: the ten-syllable last line fits the traditional syllable count but establishes a rhythm of its own. If you are not that sort of reader, that's fine: Wright leads with kinds of language, with tone of voice, not with meter, and she wants you to come along, to visit, to come right back. "Poem" could be quoting a lot of southern grandmothers (though not mine), a lot of mothers or fathers, after a long day: we have not lost our rocky perch.

Does every community require its own distinctive kind of poem or form? Maybe; maybe not. James Weldon Johnson is most often mentioned today for his satirical novel *Autobiography of an Ex-Colored Man* and for his pioneering free verse in the voice of an African American preacher, collected as *God's Trombones*. Johnson also wrote more conventional metered verse, including the words to "Lift Ev'ry Voice and Sing" (1900), sung at formal occasions by African Americans throughout the twentieth century:

> Stony the road we trod,
> Bitter the chastening rod,
> Felt in the days when hope unborn had died;
> Yet with a steady beat,
> Have not our weary feet
> Come to the place for which our fathers sighed?

Yet Johnson was not content with that kind of inherited form; much later, in 1922, he wrote that "what the colored [African American] poet in the United States needs to do is something like [what John Millington] Synge did for the Irish; he needs to find a form that will express the racial spirit by symbols from within, rather than by symbols from without." Johnson was calling, in effect, for the Harlem Renaissance, for the flourishing of new and distinctively African American styles in the 1920s, in poets such as Jean Toomer and Langston Hughes. Black poets, of course, have not stopped trying to find new forms, some of them (like Fred Moten's, which we saw in chapter 4) distinctively tied to Black experience.

Other modern poets have created new forms by trying to represent their communities' patterns of language use, from polyglot vocabularies to distinctive writing systems. A wonderful recent example is the slateku, a form invented by the Deaf and visually impaired poet and critic John Lee Clark. The form's haiku-like brevity depends on the number of characters and on the complex puns made possible by the portable mechanical braille slate, on which many words become other words if you turn the slate over or write them in reverse. The poems are in effect always translations, not between languages but between writing systems, and they lose something (but not everything) when they are spoken out loud or printed in flat ink. Here is one:

> When we say good morning
> In Japanese Sign Language
> We pull down a string
> To greet each other in a new light

And here is another:

> Prehistory
> The French army wanted to talk
> In the dark
> Without making a sound

Braille really did evolve out of a French army code; Charles Barbier created a "night writing" during the Napoleonic Wars before Louis Braille adapted it for blind people. Other slateku have subjects unrelated to disability. But they are always, also, emblems of community, ways of using language to make poems that only somebody acquainted with braille can wholly understand; as surely as Manhire's poems about New Zealand, or Niedecker's about the rural Midwest, Clark's slateku say several things for several communities, imagining overlapping ways of feeling and thinking for each one.

Other poems and poets at least try to speak about matters common to all human beings. All of us have bodies, for example, and each of us will at some point die. Wallace Stevens's "A Postcard from the Volcano," adapting its figures from Herculaneum and Pompeii, works through a range of emotions about the fact that all human endeavors end. "Children picking up our bones / Will never know that these were once / As quick as foxes on the hill," Stevens begins, in emphatic, unusual four-beat lines (it's hard to keep up a four-beat, seven- or eight-syllable line for long in English without the support of rhyme). We all become bones, Stevens knows; all walls will be ruins. Every civilization falls. And yet (Stevens muses) even the poems, and the other art, that gets forgotten may change how the world of the future feels, may have left some potentially permanent mark. "We knew for long the mansion's look / And what we said of it became / A part of what it is," though future children "will speak our speech and never know."

That "we" means, for Stevens, each, or any, generation; for Dana Levin it means everyone right now. Her recent book *Banana Palace* works hard to generalize, in terse, quotable ways, not about her own experience merely but about her sense of our era, of the way we live together—or fail to live together—in 2018:

Mine was the era
of spending your time
   in town squares made out of air.

You invented a face
   and moved it around, visited briefly
   with other faces. . . .

Information about information was the pollen we
deposited—
   while in the real fields bees starved.

The poem envisions a failure of community, or else a collective failure on the part of a human community to notice and
care for the nonhuman world. And it does so with an almost
stately pace, as if Levin were making sure her alarm did not
lead her to panic, lest she cause her readers to panic too.

The fact that we die, and the fact that works of art (like
Stevens's, like Clark's, like Levin's) preserve experiences that
might otherwise go away for good, can become the basis for
a feeling of human community, a sense of continuity, and not
only in one Stevens poem. Here is Ryszard Krynicki again, in
Clare Cavanagh's translation:

A crow's cuneiform on the snow:
I'm not extinct.
You who read this

aren't either.

Sumerian cuneiform letters on clay tablets have survived long
after Sumeria; our poems, or some of them, may do likewise,

even when we ourselves are as long vanished as Sumeria, or as melting snow.

Stevens's poem, like Krynicki's, aspires to be, or to sound, universal; Levin's, to speak for everyone alive, or everyone literate, at a particular moment. Civilizations fall, walls collapse, snow melts, in Baltimore and in Bhutan, Brussels and Brunei. That does not mean every poet can, or should, aspire to speak to everyone. Experiences shared largely or only by Baltimoreans, or by girls, or by engineers, might produce just as powerful a poem as experiences that might be shared by us all; if we are not engineers or were never girls, we might not belong to the community that the poem addresses, though we can read and love it anyway. Layli Long Soldier's tremendously influential recent book *Whereas* includes a sequence of prose poems in which the poet contemplates her own need for community, her entanglement with a larger community that might include human and nonhuman life. That community is not the set of all human beings, though, but the set of Lakota speakers, or else a larger commonality among Native nations. "WHEREAS I did not desire in childhood to be a part of this," Long Soldier writes, "but desired most of all to be a part. A piece combined with others to make up a whole. Some but not all of something. In Lakota it's hanjké, a piece or part of anything. Like the creek trickling behind my aunt's house where Uncle built her a bridge to cross from bank to bank."

Long Soldier's long, elaborate title poem mixes such personal recollection—often inside a single sentence—with the language of lawyers' and elected officials' pronouncements, among them President Barack Obama's 2009 apology to Native Americans for centuries of displacement. Such pronouncements are not enough, can never be enough, to make up for the past. Long Soldier speaks simultaneously to herself, to members of her nation and other Native nations, and to non-Native people who may not already know or feel that "Native people as in tribes as in people living over *there* are people with their own nation each with its own government and flag they rise and sing in their own languages, even. And by *there* I mean *here* all around us." Long Soldier also writes verse, but her prose is aggressively not the language of exposition, of documentation, of unadorned narrative: it's a highly charged prose poem, one whose nonstandard usage heightens the passion, and the frustration, that it presents.

Long Soldier's use of Lakota—like Herrera's use of Spanish and *pocho* (Chicanx/Mexican American) Spanish, Craig Santos Perez's use of Chamoru, or Tibble's use of te reo Māori—is no accident. These poets' polyglot or multilingual works signal multiple kinds of belonging; the signal succeeds if the poem does, not as a simple announcement but as a work of art. And of course some important American poetry of community, identity, and solidarity is not written in English at all. Nor is it necessarily written down. Kao Kalia Yang's astonishing memoir *The Song Poet* describes her immigrant father Bee Yang's success in Minnesota as a poet of *kwv txhiaj*, Hmong-language song poetry, shared in live performances and through "cassettes in local Hmong grocery stores": "In his song," Yang recalls, "I was one with a people who had lived for a long time, traveled across many lands, a people clinging to each other for a reminder, a promise, of home, that place deep inside and far beyond where the Hmong people had hidden in our hearts." Nor was such a response one daughter's alone: "After my father's song ended, there was a stretch of silence . . . and then the echoing ring of applause. Men and women rushed toward him at the stage's edge and they clapped their hands on his back." Many traditions, many languages, have nurtured such poets, such composers of verse that sustains one or another community, whether or not it turns up in English in books like my own right now.

•

Every poem comes out of at least one tradition, at least one set of models in earlier poems. Most poems have multiple identifiable models, whether in *kwv txhiaj* or in John Milton. You don't have to know all, or any, of those traditions and models to like or enjoy or find yourself moved by one poem. Every poem could potentially be someone's first, though some work better for newbies than others. Once you no longer feel like a newbie, though, you might want to try to account for traditions, for how a poem speaks to its own and its readers' history. T. S. Eliot's 1919 essay "Tradition and the Individual Talent" works very strenuously to disentangle the story of poems from the story of poets: poetry is "not the expression of personality but an escape from personality," Eliot insists, though he adds, with characteristic coyness, "Only those who have personality and emotions know what it means to want to escape from those things." He also implies (though he qualifies the claim elsewhere) that the only poems worth caring about are major ones, "monuments" that "form an existing order among themselves," an order that changes when a new monument (perhaps on a flatbed truck) gets hauled in.

Such monumental models (canons, if you like) can be useful guides but also (sometimes inadvertent) bullies, discouraging you from reading widely, from loving obscurity, from figuring out what you really like, as against what you're supposed to like or what will be on the test. These monumental models can also make the history of poetry look like a very long single-elimination tournament, a series of duels or wrestling matches where writers compete to be remembered or to exercise authority. The critic Walter Jackson Bate noticed, in *The Burden of the Past and the English Poet* (1970), that many poets during the 1700s and 1800s worried themselves half sick about how much good verse had already been written: How could writers of the present day compete? During the 1960s and 1970s the literary critic Harold Bloom converted such Romantic worries—along with a large dose of Freudian psychology—into a whole theory by which true poets, or strong poets, had to compete with and defeat their de facto poetic fathers, transforming and overthrowing old ways of writing almost as a rebel (Milton, say) might overthrow a king.

Bloom and Bate were on to something. We can, if we want, see literary history as a kind of struggle for control of the language, or a struggle to stop echoing somebody else, to find your own signature or your own voice. Poets, like every other kind of artist, begin by imitation; sooner or later ambitious ones try to stop copying. (Even the radical poets who want to sound like a collective, not like individual human beings, are trying to do something not already accomplished by other collectives.) And—as Bloom noticed—later poets can take over our sensibility or control our account of literary history. We read earlier poems—just as we read about the historical past—in ways affected by what came next.

And yet, to those who have seen (for example) the film *Black Panther*, the Bloomian vision of poetry as an endless struggle for preeminence, a series of fights between poetic sons and their fathers, may seem as fascinatingly obsolete as the ritual combat of Wakanda's kings. The territory of poetry is not a monarchy, not a single territory, not an exclusive inheritance, and it is not ordinarily at war.

There are better ways to see poetic community, history, and tradition. One has less to do with what happens in *Black Panther* than it does with the people who went to see it. Some of those people knew all about Wakanda from the comics; other people (more of them) were encountering most of these stories for the first time. Some people saw the film again and again. Some found a special resonance in that film or felt as if it had been made for them. And some went home to draw pictures of T'Challa and Shuri, Okoye and Bucky, to tell stories about them or act them out; a few, perhaps more than a few, will go on to write comics or make feature films. They have joined a shared universe with a history of references, technical moves, visual and aural cues, and characters that they—and we—can learn to recognize.

That's what it means to enter a social life organized around an art form, one that includes both a big, splashy public side and a whole bundle of things most people don't recognize (and may not care to recognize). That's why the history of an art form can generate, and sustain, its own communities. You can see this kind of sociability, this shared investment in works drawn from other works, not just in feature films about comic-book heroes but in other art forms too: poems make up one of those art forms, or rather (even if you look only at poems in English) dozens of them, with shared roots and divergent branches. Learning the history of poetry, learning to feel comfortable in it, perhaps writing, sharing, and revising your own poems, is less like a struggle to become the Black Panther than it is like becoming a *Black Panther* fan. It is even more like becoming a Marianne Moore fan, or climbing into a giant family tree, one with multiple roots, thick trunks, and intertwining branches, like a baobab. People who care, and have cared, for that tree, people who have climbed it and tried to live there, are not exactly a recognized demographic, like Deaf people or Pennsylvania voters. And yet we, too, are a community, or rather many overlapping communities; we, too, persist over time, and some of us are also Deaf, or vote in Pennsylvania, or liked *Black Panther* and want to write comic books now.

Poems can refer to the history of poetry—and hence to the history of many communities—through a shared form that persists over time: terza rima, or sonnets, or the Golden Shovel (all discussed in chapter 3). Poems can also make use of their own history by quoting, or answering, particular earlier poems, like Twitter threads that go back thousands of years. Some poets make those answers explicit, building entire poems around them. Monica Youn concludes her 2016 volume *Blackacre* with a fourteen-part prose poem that responds, line by line, to the line-ending words in John Milton's Sonnet 19, "On His Blindness." Milton begins "When I consider how my light is spent"; Youn asks why Milton would consider light, or sight, or time on earth, his own to hoard or spend: "'Spent'—a word like a flapping sack. . . . My mistake was similar. I came to consider my body—its tug-of-war of taut-nesses and slacknesses—to be entirely my own, an appliance for generating various textures and temperatures of friction. Should I have known, then, that by this act of self-claiming, I was cutting myself off from the eternal, the infinite?" Milton was writing in the seventeenth century about his eyesight, his piety, and his labor; Youn is writing in the 2010s about fertility and infertility, competing claims to a woman's body in particular, and, also, about Milton. Her prose is both poetry and literary criticism, and it gets its force, like a maglev train, by rising above, repelling, keeping its fixed distance from Milton's sturdy words.

Youn puts her grapple with Milton right up front. More often, though, poems talk back to earlier poems, and to the groups of people who care for those poems, through what Marvel-movie viewers and gamers call Easter eggs, delightful or ironic aspects visible only to those prepared to see. Maureen McLane's book *Some Say* (2017) works hard to seem open to any literate reader: its short-lined, frequently rhymed poems can aspire to the effects of folk song. It also talks back, grate-fully, to poems from other eras. Her book title refers to Emily Dickinson's plea (first published, as prose, in a posthumous collection of her letters, in 1894) that her poems be read aloud:

A word is dead
When it is said
Some say
I say it just
Begins to live
That day.

McLane's title also invokes the ancient Greek poem by Sappho (called, by classicists, Fragment 16) that gives McLane a model for her own erotic verse. McLane's title poem begins as a free translation of Sappho and then veers off:

Some say a host
of horsemen, a horizon
of ships under sail
is most beautiful &
some say a mountain
embraced by the clouds &
some say the badass
booty-shakin' shorties
in the club are most
beautiful and some say
the truth is most
beautiful. . . .
   I say
what they say
is sometimes
what I say
Her legs long
and bare shining
on the bed

Hers is a vision of girls and women together, of literally Sapphic tradition, partly lighthearted and partly serious: queer women across time and space, in McLane's vision, might form our own fleet of ships, our own fierce host.

These overt rewrites of earlier famous poems do not just show that writers in the present have something in common with the past. They also show that the past belongs to us, that we can find our people in it, with proper allowance for their difference from us; we are like them in some ways, though never in all. Patience Agbabi's contemporary rewrite of Chaucer's *Canterbury Tales* includes not only a drastically shortened, and delightful, "Franklin's Tale" but her own version of Chaucer's "General Prologue," whose famous original version (in Middle English) begins:

> When that Aprille with his shoures soote
> The droghte of March hath perced to the roote
> And bathed every veine in swich licour
> Of which virtú engendred is the flour...

In modern English:

> When April with his sweet showers
> Has pierced the dryness of March to the root
> And bathed every vein in the liquid
> Whose distinctive power makes flowers grow...

It's a classic early instance of that distinctively English thing, iambic pentameter ("perced" is pronounced "peer-said," "bathed," "bah-thed," to preserve the even count of ten syllables and five beats). Agbabi's updated Chaucerian host speaks in an unmistakable hip-hop cadence instead, with two strong beats concluding every line:

> When my April showers me with kisses
> I could make her my missus or my mistress

but I'm happily hitched—sorry home girls—
said my vows to the sound of the Bow Bells
yet her breath is as fresh as the west wind,
when I breathe her, I know we're predestined.

"The Bow Bells" are in working-class East London. The verse is an update, an homage, a manifestation of literary community across time and space, and a reason to read the old poem together with the new: the update lets readers join this community too.

You don't have to be medieval to enjoy Chaucer, any more than you have to be British, or Nigerian, or a Londoner, to get into Agbabi (and I certainly hope you don't have to be a trans white Jewish American college professor to read me). If you start to think about literary history, though—about the communities that poets make possible, about who can join them, and how, and when, and why—you will have to think about who gets the chance to speak and publish and write, and why, and on what terms. Too often, school-approved literary history has placed (whether or not the teachers intended to do so) white, rich, urban, cisgender men at the center, treating their experience as universal and other poets as special cases. The monumental unfairness of Western history, including literary history, is no reason to stop reading Keats (who was far from rich), but it is a reason to ask—as poets interested in community and tradition have had to ask—how a literary community, and a literary history, a history not just of authors but of styles and ways to read, looks if you put (for example) Caribbean writers, or people who grew up poor, or women raising young children, at its center.

That last example might look like Bernadette Mayer's *Midwinter Day*. The book-length poem, like James Joyce's *Ulysses*, takes place over the course of a single day, in this case December 22, 1978, a day that the poet spent with her two young children in their artsy but threadbare town in the mountains of western Massachusetts. The poem's six segments in verse and prose explore and extend Mayer's many kinds of connections: to other writers, past and present; to her then partner, the poet Lewis Warsh, and their young kids; to her potential readers, present and future; and to other mothers all over the place:

> Wisdom's wives and children
> Surround the town like hills all alone like soldiers
> It's quiet, there's the air
>   In the important post office
> We open Box 718 which is a drawer like the morgue,
> People are either smiling or mad because of Xmas
> There's another birthday card for Sophia from Julius and Julia
> A Penny Saver, a bank statement and a bill from Weleda,
> No letters checks or invitations change the world
> Lewis closes the mail drawer and drops his glasses,
> One of the lenses flies out, he throws up his hands
>   And says
> "What's the use?" Then Marie trips over her own boots
> And hits her head on a brick
>   Sophia's mittens come off,
> The disappearing scene from a dream I remember is lost
> To comparisons of past exertion for the slight Main Street hill,
> I blink at seeing, being seen a little
>   I wonder why we write at all
> These trees have seen this all before
> But they are glad of an encore

Amiably exasperated by the needs of a household and children, and by a man who seemingly cannot take care of himself, or even keep track of his glasses, Mayer feels "seen a little." The poem itself—rambling, anecdotal, alternately comic and rapt—imagines a community, imagines ways we might see one another, in ways that no laconic lyric, no elegant narrative, could. At times *Midwinter Day* feels almost like a metaphor for the shared childcare and neighborhood-wide shared parenting that so many new parents (more often than not, mothers) crave. "I am like a woman who says I am another woman," Mayer writes later, "or a man who says I am another man"; her sense of herself, as manifest in this open-ended, almost faux-naïf poem, cannot be severed from her potential connections to you, and you, and you.

Mayer did not always write in this fluent, almost awkward, pellucid way. Her earlier poetry is extraordinarily challenging, even bizarre, often meant to evade prose sense. The language poets we saw in chapter 4 saw her as an ally, or as a precedent. *Midwinter Day* emerged not just from her motherhood but from her relocation to the Berkshires in Massachusetts, away from New York and from her changed sense of who she was writing *for*: no longer a group of anti-academic, cutting-edge (or would-be cutting-edge) downtown writers and artists, but someone else: perhaps her close friends, perhaps mothers or other parents, who could be living anywhere.

Other poets have also altered their styles and goals when they changed their sense of community, of what groups they might write for. Mayer makes one good example; Gwendolyn Brooks makes another. Brooks became the first African American woman to win a Pulitzer Prize, in 1950, for

Annie Allen; she said that she assembled its impressive array of work, most with rhyme and meter, "to prove to others (by implication, not by shouting) and to such among themselves who have yet to discover it, that they are merely human beings, not exotics." While she wrote self-consciously elaborate poems for, and about, adults, she also wrote about, and for, Black children, naming her book of children's poetry after her own neighborhood on Chicago's West Side, *Bronzeville Boys and Girls*. In 1967, a famous and disputatious conference about Black writing at Fisk University solidified Brooks's sense that the world had changed, that Black nationalism was the way forward. Her work became more fragmented, more jagged, and stranger to fit the unsettled times, and then, after about 1970, far more direct, simpler in its patterns and in its choice of words, as if she were taking special care not to exclude any Black reader of any age: "My aim, in my next future, is to write poems that will somehow successfully 'call' all black people," she announced. She wanted to see "the Black Nation / defining its own Roof," and chose to publish only with Black-owned presses from the mid-1970s until her death in 2000.

My own favorite poems by Brooks all come from the late 1960s, from her transitional period, when she was trying to figure out where, if anywhere, her writing fit. Like many other observers, she thought at least some of the violence of the late 1960s might be a prelude to a better social order. She could see a figure like the boy in "Boy Breaking Glass" (a poem she read to an audience at the Fisk conference) not only as an agent of chaos but as the voice of an unheard community. This boy

Whose broken window is a cry of art
(success, that winks aware
as elegance, as a treasonable faith)
is raw: is sonic: is old-eyed première.
Our beautiful flaw and terrible ornament.
Our barbarous and metal little man.

He is as confounding, as hard to interpret, as the historical cir-
cumstances that led him to throw his brick or rock, to smash
the window in which he could not see himself.

Brooks is one of those poets (Auden is another) whom
various readers have various, even contradictory, reasons for
liking, and for liking the same poems. If this book works as
I hope it will, you will evolve your own reasons for liking
poems too, however you find more of them (in anthologies,
on websites, in single-author volumes, via audio or video):
they will be reasons not wholly congruent with my own six
categories (feeling, character, technique, difficulty, wisdom,
and community). That's one reason (and not the only one)
why this book does not conclude with directions for further
reading, nor with a glossary of technical terms: where you
go, and what you want to learn when you get there, will
differ so much from traveler to traveler in the vast territories
of dissimilar texts and performances that we call poems. The
more you learn about poetic techniques—about what rhyme
can do, how line breaks work, about the uses of zeugma and
anthimeria and a thousand other techniques that you might
recognize and enjoy without ever looking up the names for
them—the more you can like, and the more you will be able
to say about what you like and why.

And if you look at those conversations—over recent years or over centuries—you may find a pattern, one that reflects the ways in which (to quote Rachel Hartman again) we are all of us more than one thing. We have seen poets compare themselves to particular things (James Merrill's mirror, for example, or Elizabeth Bishop's giant toad): we have also seen poets say that they are many things at once, as if to show how we, too, might be multiple. And we can see poets acknowledging that the same poem, the same poet, might serve many purposes, please many readers for many reasons, unlock our hearts with any one of many keys. Kasischke suggests as much in a poem called "Riddle":

I am the mirror breathing above the sink.
There is a censored garden inside of me.
Over my worms someone has thrown

a delicately embroidered sheet.

And also the child at the rummage sale—

more souvenirs than memories.

I am the cat buried beneath
the tangled ivy. Also the white
weightless egg
floating over its grave.

Each of these objects can be one figure for what a poem does, one reason to read some poems: a poem may be a mirror that shows you your own face, a way to meet an imaginary character, a craft object that serves as a memorial, a magical thing like a levitating egg, an imagined new birth. Can the same poem be, or seem to be, all those things?

The TV chef Alton Brown likes to say that his kitchens have (with one exception) no single-taskers, no implements, like a grapefruit spoon, that will do only one thing. The limited space on his shelves is, instead, reserved for tools that can accomplish many tasks in many recipes: skewers, slotted spoons, a quality knife. You could say the same thing about the mental "shelf space" that we reserve for our favorite poems. Some poems become famous fast, or matter a great deal to certain readers, because they're so good at just one thing, like a fire extinguisher (Brown's one exception). But the poems that stick around for decades or centuries, the poems that outlast typewriters and survive revolutions, are usually more like pans and knives: they can speak to many readers in many ways, have many uses, can do many things.

Some of those poems are long: *Paradise Lost*, for example. Others are famously compact, easy to memorize, known for single central symbols: Dickinson's "Split the Lark—and you'll find the Music," with its caution against overinterpretation, or Wallace Stevens's "Anecdote of the Jar," which is also an answer to Keats's urn, or Brooks's "We Real Cool." Adrienne Rich created such streamlined emblems too, in poems whose single symbol rockets them into readers' memories, as in "Prospective Immigrants Please Note":

> Either you will
> go through this door
> or you will not go through.

If you go through
there is always the risk
of remembering your name.

More often one poem gives many people many reasons to read it, reasons that encompass more than one of the six categories that this book has tried to advance. Brooks's "Boy Breaking Glass" is at once a cascade of spectacular mysterious metaphors, a lattice of irregular rhymes, a display of craft; a portrait of a violently dissatisfied young character; and a warning, addressed from and to a community, about coming chaos or incipient revolution. Revard's "What the Eagle Fan Says" is both an emblem of communal continuity, of what some Native writers call "survivance," and a show of verse form. "Tintern Abbey" is a poem that delves into confusion, but it's also a source of wisdom and a way to portray some very intricate feelings.

Most of the poems that survive, that accumulate critics and fans over decades and centuries, work like that: they do more than one thing for more than one set of readers, and they do things I have tried to describe in more than one of the six chapters here. Some even do all six of those things. I'll end with two such poems, one from the twentieth century, one a bit older. First, Rich's "Power," from 1978:

Living   in the earth-deposits   of our history

Today a backhoe divulged   out of a crumbling flank of earth
one bottle   amber   perfect   a hundred-year-old
cure for fever   or melancholy   a tonic

for living on this earth   in the winters of this climate

Today I was reading about Marie Curie:
she must have known she suffered   from radiation sickness
her body bombarded for years   by the element
she had purified
It seems she denied to the end
the source of the cataracts on her eyes
the cracked and suppurating skin   of her finger-ends
till she could no longer hold   a test-tube or a pencil

She died a famous woman   denying
her wounds
denying
her wounds came   from the same source as her power

This poem, I think, will last for a very long time, not just because it means a great deal to me (and it has meant various things at various times) but because it contains—as well as describes, explains, even excavates and preserves—the power to mean many things, to do many things, for many readers, or for one reader at successive encounters.

"Power" has been, from its first publication, a kind of manifesto for disempowered groups, a call to dig for our own usable past. Rich invites us to join her in her defiance, in her resolution, in her determination to work through pain; she seeks, as we seek, a tonic for these tough times. Rich uses midline spaces to indicate pauses shorter or less meaningful than a line break; as in Carter Revard's Eagle Fan riddle, the device calls back to Anglo-Saxon alliterative verse with its frequently martial or stoic attitude, its consonant-rich lines.

It should be clear already how the poem shares feelings—of dispossession, unease, joyful recovery—and how it offers wisdom or advice.

That advice, though, might change as you reread. Curie kept working even as it killed her, through the grotesque pain that Rich's word choice ("suppurating" in particular) carries. Did Curie know what she was doing? Did she make a mistake? Did she decide, calmly or after much anguish, that it was worth an even more painful death from radiation poisoning if she could do more laboratory work before she died? Rich's poem is not, exactly, an overt display of skill with inherited forms, like a sestina or an anagram; it is, however, a kind of tribute to technique, to the skill sets and the concentration that let lab scientists, and poets, do their work, creating "perfect" objects, things that might last or "cure."

Or kill. The harder you look at the poem, the more ambivalent, or difficult, it becomes. Both Curie and the backhoe operators have found ineffective or dangerous "cures." (Radium tonics and fad treatments really did kill people in the early twentieth century.) What to do with a dangerous discovery? What to do if you get your power from a dangerous or misguided practice, or from a talent that could be used for ill, or from an establishment—say, a cis male–dominated, white-run poetry world—that does not have your interests at heart? "Power" ends up—among many other things—not only as a call to create community, to unearth and display and take pride in our wounds and our power, but also as a kind of warning from Rich to herself, and to writers like her, not to forget where we derive that power, not to speak only for ourselves.

Rich for much her life suffered—her later poems record her suffering—from rheumatoid arthritis; her son gave arthritis as her cause of death. She may have seen herself not only in Curie's pioneering fame but also in her trembling, painful fingers. Those of us with other impairments, other physical or social challenges, may see ourselves there too. Almost anyone who has taken a creative writing class has heard the mantra "Write what you know." Rich says instead, with Curie as ironic evidence, "Write from what hurts you; investigate what gives you pain; seek your community there." Feeling and character, form and difficulty, wisdom and community: all here.

The history in "Power" is not just the half-buried history of material objects, of patent medicine, of radiation science, and of women's struggle to be seen. It is, too, the history of poetry, since Rich virtually quotes several earlier poems. Her "perfect" bottle recalls Stevens's "Anecdote of the Jar" ("I placed a jar in Tennessee") and, through Stevens, Keats's "Ode on a Grecian Urn." Jesus told Peter that he would deny him three times before the cock crowed; Rich uses some form of "deny" three times as well. "Deny deny deny / is not all the roosters cry," wrote Elizabeth Bishop in "Roosters," an antiwar poem Rich might also have had in mind. Finally, that backhoe and its "crumbling earth," leaving "us" unsure about public affairs, also echo the "dinosaur steamshovels" in Robert Lowell's then well-known poem about personal and political helplessness, "For the Union Dead" (1960). Lowell's poem concludes with a kind of flailing despair as he watches the civil rights struggle on TV: around him in greater Boston, "a savage servility / slides by on grease." Rich's poem of excavation and memory feels like a counter to that helplessness; wherever you are, she suggests, you can always dig there.

Poets and poems must complain, must protest, Rich implies. That is one reason we have poems. Sometimes they complain about tragic situations that have no solution, such as the fact that we change over time, age, and die. At other times, writers have been all too inclined to treat social, changeable facts as if they were natural and eternal, protests always futile, "ignorant of the fact this way of grief / is shared unnecessary / and political" (as Rich put it in her poem "Translations"). And yet the idea of complaint, the idea that poems embody problems that we have not yet solved, or do not know how to solve, can still seem central to the history of poetry, as to so many individual poems. Even the great poems of joy, love, attachment, and satisfaction (among them the poem by Frank O'Hara with which chapter 1 began) emerge from the ways in which we are shaped by pain and the ways not every joy can be shared. And the mixed feelings that Auden found at the center of every good poem, the multiple uses and multiple pleasures I have been trying to help you find in poems, so often come back either to what we can share with others—to who's listening—or to what we can make into song. Here is Gerard Manley Hopkins's sonnet "The Caged Skylark," written in 1877 and first published after the poet's death, in 1918:

As a dare-gale skylark scanted in a dull cage,
    Man's mounting spirit in his bone-house, mean house,
      dwells —
    That bird beyond the remembering his free fells;
This in drudgery, day-labouring-out life's age.

Though aloft on turf or perch or poor low stage
　　Both sing sometímes the sweetest, sweetest spells,
　　Yet both droop deadly sómetimes in their cells
Or wring their barriers in bursts of fear or rage.

Not that the sweet-fowl, song-fowl, needs no rest—
Why, hear him, hear him babble & drop down to his nest,
　　But his own nest, wild nest, no prison.

Man's spirit will be flesh-bound, when found at best,
But uncumberèd: meadow-down is not distressed
　　For a rainbow footing it nor he for his bónes rísen.

As in most of his poems, Hopkins—an English Jesuit priest who published no poetry during his adult lifetime—draws on his favorite, idiosyncratic, Scotist Catholic theology. The gorgeous language might take a few times through to decode. "Uncumbered" means "unencumbered," unrestrained; "fells" has its British meaning of steep wild places. The sense that governs the poem, that controls its end, includes (as in Shakespeare's Sonnet 116) a refutation: Hopkins is writing against the idea (we have seen it in earlier religious poems, by Samuel Johnson, Christina Rossetti, and others) that this life is nothing more than a cage, and against the idea that bodies and sensual experience (including the sensuality of language) do not matter. He may also be responding to the caged bird in Tennyson's *In Memoriam*, the bird we saw in chapter 5.

The spirit, for Hopkins, does not regret the flesh; rather, the spirit strains against this world, this body, this society, because it can and will find for itself a better flesh, a better set of senses, after the Second Coming (in Hopkins's Catholic theology) or simply in the future somewhere. Hopkins's own syntax, similarly, finds a better, stranger, stronger form for his energies than the word order of standard spoken English. That new form invites you to share its joys, to imagine the poet who in turn sees himself in the skylark, to revel in its interplay of sounds, and to work harder than usual to follow Hopkins's complicated sense.

All of us tire; all of us want nests, limits, homes of some kind, no matter how much or how often we dare to fly through storms. The limits and the shapes the poem gives Hopkins's sentiments—very much unlike the cage for the songbird—are the shapes the poem itself requires, its "wild nest" no prison imposed from outside. In the same way, for Hopkins (who is, as usual, both pious and sensuous), the body itself is no prison; the horizon does not confine the rainbow but rather permits it to rise. These lines combine the overall shape of the sonnet, with its armature of rhymes, with the repeated alliteration that Hopkins takes from Anglo-Saxon and Welsh verse. These features join an insistence on something like freedom, for bodies as well as for minds. The sonnet speaks at once to Catholic versions of the resurrection and to the hopes being articulated, across the Atlantic Ocean in the same decade, for huddled masses yearning to breathe free.

I began writing this book about how to read poetry in the spring of 2015, in the United States, when the dominant conversations around American poetry had begun to shift from sometimes abstract arguments about language, meaning, and sense toward questions about race and audience, about how to hear new voices and performance traditions, and about structural social problems that poems alone could never solve. I took the book—and its focus—to New Zealand and Britain and back; I conclude in the fall of 2018, when representatives of the United States government are confining immigrant children in desert camps. Poetry cannot on its own end such atrocities, nor can we ask it to do so. It will not upend our system of government, nor will it alter many 51–49 votes in any legislature.

And yet its effects on people—and not just on me—are real. The reasons that we have for reading and rereading one or another poem—for its shared feelings, for its sense of other people's humanity, for its demonstration of what human beings can make and do—are, at least some of the time, the same reasons we pay attention to real other people, alone or in groups. The caged skylark is also the tragic caged soul, trapped in one body as long as they both shall live, but it is also, might be, the caged citizen, despondent and downcast for a night or a year, and yet attentive as long as somebody can hear. A poem is not a vote, and yet there are reasons both poems and votes get compared to the human voice. We have seen poems as songs from cells and prisons, poems as representative animals, poems as displays of technique, poems as ways to think about what's hard to say, poems as wisdom, poems as solidarity with others, and poems as links to the history of an art: Hopkins's skylark, like Rich's backhoe and tonic, invokes all of these ways to read, these reasons to read. You can adopt, or adapt, Hopkins's poem if you like, as a protest against unnecessary imprisonment, or take it as something that hopes to survive its own time: as a celebratory pushback against tragic outlooks, a promise that we will resist even those limits (death, for example) that no words, no forms, and no social change can defeat. The soul comes out in the poem, and continues to sing.

ACKNOWLEDGMENTS

A book of this kind could not be undertaken—let alone completed—without the many hands that make light work, nor without multiple sources of friendship, patience, and companionship, nor without good advice from more than one friendly expert in more than one field. I am grateful to my editor, Lara Heimert, and to her colleagues at Basic Books, to Jeff Shotts and the rest of the pack at Graywolf, to my book agent, Matt McGowan, to my agents at Blue Flower (especially Anya Backlund), as well as to the many living poets who offered their words and looked at parts of the book; some of those poets also gave us permission to quote their poems. I'm thankful to Harvard University and to my department chairs and dean there, Robin Kelsey, James Simpson, and Nicholas Watson, and to Paul Millar and the University of Canterbury in Christchurch, Aotearoa/New Zealand. My thanks to the assiduous and generous Virginia-based correspondent who sent proposed corrections for the paperback editions: their name has been lost to the COVID work-from-home era and to an office move, but their insights remain. I'm grateful too, in many ways and for many reasons, to Jordan Ellenberg, Rachel Gold, Laura Kinney, Carmen Giménez Smith, Rachel Trousdale, verity, and Monica Youn, as well as to the other friends, writers, and editors who offered so much during the relevant years; a list of them all would take up more than one page. I've been lucky enough to have the support of my parents, Sandra and Jeffrey Burt. And I am glad every day to collaborate on life's endeavors with the inimitable Jessica Bennett, and with Cooper and Nathan, all of whom can "make one little room an everywhere."

PERMISSIONS

INDEX

JESSICA BENNETT

Stephanie Burt is a professor of English at Harvard University and the recipient of a 2016 Guggenheim fellowship for poetry. Her work appears regularly in the *New York Times Book Review*, *New Yorker*, *London Review of Books*, and other journals. She has authored fourteen books of poetry and literary criticism, including *Advice from the Lights* and *The Poem Is You*. She lives in Massachusetts.